ACCOLADES

"*The Imperfect Storm* is a relatable, down-to-earth book about steps to take to ensure a secure financial foundation and a satisfying, worry-free retirement. To describe this journey to long-term financial security, author and financial advisor Derek Reed employs what is surely a unique point of view for a book about financial planning: that of a fishing boat captain. He has obviously been inspired by watching what it took for his own father to become one. To illustrate the practical steps outlined in the book, he blends stories from his father's experiences on the water with tales from his own life and the lives of some of his clients. The result is a very entertaining book full of strategies and good examples of how to align your money and values to live a life of purpose and meaning and to leave in your "wake" a legacy that touches people long after you are gone."

– Susan Turnbull, *founder and principal,*
Personal Legacy Advisors

"I've seen Derek navigate challenges in his life with wisdom and grace. This is a great book about your retirement journey, during which you may encounter challenges, too. I wholeheartedly recommend you read and apply its principles to increase your chances of smooth sailing in the years to come."

– Caleb Callahan, CFP®, CKA, CEPA, *president,*
Valmark Financial Group

"As a Gloucester fisherman's daughter and someone who has known Derek for decades, I can attest to his, his dad's, and his entire family's authenticity and grit. In addition to being long-term friends, I'm also a long-term client. As such, I've experienced the care and professionalism he brings to his work and his involvement as a respected community member. His book, *The Imperfect Storm*, puts all that and more on display as it teaches us how to navigate the potentially turbulent seas of retirement."

– *Ann-Margaret Ferrante,*
Massachusetts State Representative

"Derek masterfully navigates the waters of retirement planning, casting complex principles into clear, practical lessons. Like a seasoned fisherman, he equips readers with the tools to chart their financial course and reel in a secure future. A compelling and valuable resource for anyone ready to set sail on their retirement journey."

– *Alexander Lowry, professor of finance and executive director, Master of Science in Financial Analysis, Gordon College*

"Insightful, informative, and practical, this is a book I wish I'd had access to years ago because countless people I know would have benefitted from it. In fact, as I consider what lies ahead for me, this will be my go-to guide! An absolute must-read."

– *Sandro Forte, president of the Million Dollar Round Table Foundation*

"Derek is the proud son of Captain Charlie, a retired Gloucester sword fisherman who is a role model of giving, courage, and action. These stories of his time at sea and their relevance to financial planning will inspire you. Reading *The Imperfect Storm* will encourage you to chart your unique course for financial independence, a meaningful retirement journey, and a personal legacy even as it warms your heart."

– *Tom Guzzardo, spirit-led Top Leaders Business Coach, speaker, and author of* Building Organizations of True Excellence

June '25

Kaylea + Ben:

Enjoy this book + part of my story!

THE IMPERFECT STORM

Successfully Navigating the Seas of Retirement

Here's to smooth sailing...
I Enjoy working w/ you both.

DEREK J. REED, CFP®, CLU®, CAP®

Cheers,
Derek

The Imperfect Storm: Successfully Navigating the Seas of Retirement

Copyright © 2025 by Derek Reed

ISBN: 978-1-7378556-4-4

All rights reserved. No part of this book may be reproduced in whole or in part without written permission from the publishers, except by reviewers who may quote brief excerpts in connection with a review in a newspaper, magazine, or electronic publication; nor may any part of this book be reproduced, stored in a retrieval system, or transmitted in any form or by any means electronic, mechanical, photocopying, recording, or other, without written permission from the publisher. The advice provided by the author is based on personal and professional experience in dealing with issues surrounding financial planning and investing; however, it is not a substitute for paid professional guidance. The studies and statistics quoted are, to the best of the author's knowledge and belief, accurate. To maintain confidentiality, some names and identifying details in this account have been altered. This book is sold without warranties of any kind, express or implied, and both the author and publisher disclaim any liability, loss, or damage caused by its contents.

Cover design by Lieve Maas

Published by Incubation Press, Bend, Oregon

Fee based planning offered through Beauport Financial Services, LLC., a Massachusetts state registered investment advisor. Third-party money management offered through Valmark Advisers, Inc., an SEC Registered Investment Advisor. Securities offered through Valmark Securities Inc. Member FINRA, SIPC Beauport Financial Services, LLC is a separate entity from Valmark Securities Inc. & Valmark Advisers, Inc..

Certified Financial Board of Standards, Inc. (CFP Board) owns the certification marks CFP®, Certified Financial Planner®, and CFP® (with plaque design) in the United States, which it authorizes use of by individuals who successfully complete CFP Board's initial and ongoing certification requirements.

This material is for informational purposes only and is not intended to provide specific advice or recommendations for any individual nor does it take into account the particular investment objectives, financial situation, or needs of individual investors. This information is not intended for use as legal or tax advice. Persons should consult with their own legal or tax advisors for specific legal or tax advice.

The information provided has been derived from sources believed to be reliable but is not guaranteed as to accuracy and does not purport to be complete analysis of the material discussed. The examples given are hypothetical and for illustrative purposes only. Actual results may vary from those illustrated.

Guarantees are based on the claims-paying ability of the issuing company. Not all characteristics described will be applicable to every situation or variable annuity. Fees will vary based on the specific products and features selected and may increase after issuance up to contractual maximums. For more information about a variable annuity, including its product features, risks, charges, and expenses, please read its prospectus.

Indexes are unmanaged and do not incur fees, one cannot directly invest in an index. Past performance does not guarantee future results. Diversification does not guarantee investment returns and does not eliminate the risk of loss.

No person has been compensated for their comments and there are no conflicts of interest related to the individuals providing the testimonials or endorsements. These comments may not be representative of all client experiences.

To Mom,

You've always lived selflessly for your children and made sure that meaningful opportunities and experiences not afforded to you as a child or as a young mother of three would certainly be available for my siblings and me. There needed to be an anchor at home every time Dad pushed off to sea; Mom, you were always that stable and firm foundation. Who you are and what you stand for is grounded in goodness, love, and patience, and I am a better man because of you.

As a child, the playground swing rides at Stage Fort Park, packed lunches on the kitchen counter each school morning, and stern reprimands when needed all showed you loved us and that you cared. I felt the love then and still feel it today.

Thank you for encouraging me to dream big, to tell the truth even when it's hard, and teaching me that life isn't always easy but to work diligently anyway.

I have been blessed with many friends, coaches, teachers, relatives, mentors, and a wife who has believed in me and I've always strived to make them proud, but above all of them is you.

Mom, I dedicate this book to you as you continue to be a blessing in my life. I've recognized that the course of my great life would have been much different without your guidance, your strength, and your unconditional love. You're an amazing woman. I remain forever grateful and strive to continue to make you proud.

With immense love and respect,
Derek

"I'm a success today because I had a friend who believed in me and I didn't have the heart to let him down."

–Abraham Lincoln

ACKNOWLEDGMENTS

I WAS A RELUCTANT WRITER with little free time to think about becoming an author and seeing this project through to completion. This book wouldn't have happened without the encouragement and help of so many people. First among them is my friend, colleague, and fellow author David Rosell. He told me "You're a fool" not to share your story and immediately put me on the phone with his writing coach Linden Gross. He always checked in on me, which held me accountable, and asked what he could do to help. All of that meant a lot to me. Much respect to you for that, Dave, and thanks for pushing me to see this through even in the most challenging of times—you're a remarkable friend.

My book coach and editor, Linden Gross, you are an angel. I know I've been your toughest and longest assignment, but at long last, we did it! You kept telling me to just tell a story and that the writing would follow. You were my biggest cheerleader on this project, telling me often, "You're so close, so close. Let's get it done!" I appreciate your patience, direction, and willingness to stick with me through this, while playing psychologist along the way. I can't begin to thank you enough!

Dad, sitting down over lunch at your kitchen table to get facts and stories for each chapter was precious time well spent. To watch you light up like a Christmas tree when remembering people and events and recalling the days of both bounty and challenge at sea was my favorite part of this whole process.

Nana, you've been gone from this place for a while now, but your calm and graceful presence remains. Thank you for the continued comfort, and for sharing so many wonderful life lessons with me. See you in heaven.

To my business partner, David McKechnie, our great team, and clients at Beauport Financial Services in Gloucester, Massachusetts. Wow! Just look at what we're building, why we do it, and who we serve. It's meaningful, we're making a difference with many, and doing it together continues to be rewarding. Thank you immensely for rallying during the opportunities and the challenges, and supporting me during my health crisis with post-viral POTS that lasted several years.

Coach Tom Guzzardo, a great friend and mentor with a higher purpose than his title of business and life coach. Tom, you have been a consistent blessing and wisdom provider since we first met five years ago. I thank you for helping me to develop my faith, my purpose, and my wisdom in a compassionate and impactful way.

To the Valmark Financial Group family and especially my annual practice builder study group brethren. You all are such seasoned, inspirational, and wise businessmen with big hearts for service and sharing. I know I receive lots of ideas and encouragement from our time together each year; I hope that this book adds something of value as part of my contribution.

As in life, it takes a team of folks to make great things happen. Publishing a book is no different, so a big thank-you goes to Lieve Maas, Kelly Byrd, and Keri-Rae Barnum for their great help with designing, editing, and publishing this book.

My family continues to be my greater purpose. Karen, Nate, Jeremy, and Katherine, you represent my North Star, and I aim to serve you all just as well as you support and love me. You all amaze me with your love, compassion, and perseverance. I love you and appreciate that you constantly seek stories at the dinner table about family, friends, and my life experiences. (Maybe that's because I always fell asleep reading books at nighttime when you were younger.) Thank you for bringing out the author buried deep inside me. *Un abrazo fuerte!*

I may be forgetting to name someone and seek your grace if so. Please know that any time you asked me how things were going with this book, provided an encouraging word, or just said good luck with this process, it mattered, and I am filled with gratitude.

Finally, here's to the nonprofits in the Cape Ann area, as well as across the globe, who are doing the work that's so desperately needed. A percentage of any revenue derived from this book—including sales and public speaking engagements—will be donated to charity.

With tremendous humility and respect for all of you,
Derek

TABLE OF CONTENTS

Introduction	1
Chapter 1 *Discovering Your Why? Assets with a Purpose*	11
Chapter 2 *Every Financial Ship Needs a Captain—Choosing Yours*	29
Chapter 3 *Charting Your Course*	59
Chapter 4 *Oceans of Opportunity and Risk*	95
Chapter 5 *If You Don't Stand For Something, You Fall for Everything*	133
Chapter 6 *Fish On! The Need to Adapt*	155
Chapter 7 *Steaming Back Home & Taking Stock*	191
Chapter 8 *The Wake Behind Your Boat: Your Legacy and Values*	229
Conclusion	253
About the Author	259

INTRODUCTION

You're thinking about a meaningful retirement. I have four questions for you.

1. Are you ready financially and emotionally?
2. Do you have an income plan?
3. What's your desired number?
4. Will your accumulated wealth support and outlive you?

It's time to address the elephant in the room. On average, some 10,000 Americans every day are reaching full retirement age, a statistic that is expected to hold until about 2033. If you are a healthy 62-year-old couple in the United States and neither of you smokes or is diabetic, one of you has over a 50 percent chance of living 30 more years. Wow! And yet, the average working American between the ages of 55 and 64 has a retirement savings balance of just $185,000 according to the *Federal Reserve's 2022 Survey* of *Consumer Finances*. Even with Social Security, that's not going to get the job done, especially given the six financial risks that every retiree faces. We'll be talking about those—and how to manage them—in the upcoming chapters. For now, let's just say that life—along with inflation and taxes—happens while we're making other plans, especially if we live for a long time.

Here's the other piece we're up against. Whether you have a savings and/or retirement plan in place or not, the financial seas not only *can* get rough, they're also *guaranteed* to get rough. Our economic reality almost ensures that another financial storm is brewing. Even though the stock market is in positive territory three out of every four years, since 1945, we've averaged a negative year in the stock market every three to four years and have hit a Category 5 storm—known as a recession—every six to seven years, where we have a stock market drop of 20 percent or worse for two quarters in a row or longer.

We don't know exactly when these reversals of fortune are going to occur, but we do know that we must be prepared for them, so they don't seriously throw us off course at a point in time when we're close to retiring or in retirement. My dad, fishing Captain Charlie Reed, taught me just that—setbacks do happen, but we can weather the storm.

Captain Charlie skippered the Andrea Gail—the boat that went down in a perfect storm in October 1991—through many a gale, experiencing in the process both profitable swordfishing trips as well as some "brokers." By the grace of God, he avoided that "perfect storm"—chronicled in Sebastian Junger's bestselling book and movie by the same name—since he had retired from swordfishing four months earlier. So, he can only guess why the 72-foot longliner sank during that historic tempest in the Northeast. Still, he knew enough about swordfishing and the Andrea Gail to be sought out as a consultant for the filmmakers.

A canvas display of Les Hagy's photo of the Andrea Gail, taken in August 1988.

Dad, a humble, now-retired commercial fishing captain out of Gloucester, Massachusetts, didn't wake up one morning and decide that he wanted to be a sword captain. Actually, swordfishing found him in the early 1980s, at a time when he was searching for greater financial opportunity to provide for his young family. Swordfishing and the alluring hunt for treasure in the wide-open North Atlantic gave him his reason and purpose. He could see and had heard of paychecks from a single month-long trip that were as much as he was then making in six months working his hourly wage job at the cold storage facility. He knew he could always go back to moving frozen fish around on pallets—solid hours and steady pay but unattractive and not lucrative enough with five mouths to feed at home. As a result, he was willing to run the risk of getting skunked (i.e., no paycheck at all) in return for the potential of a big payday.

Bob Brown, the owner of the Andrea Gail, trusted and placed great faith in my dad to run the boat for him and his fishing business. Dad had to plan for the month-long journeys out to the rich fishing area of the Grand Banks. He had to hire, train, and manage a competent crew; maintain a good, safe ship; meticulously review plans and inventory before heading out to sea; adapt and make numerous critical decisions while at sea; and get everyone including the treasured catch back to port safely. In essence, my dad, Captain Charlie Reed, was the first successful business owner I knew quite well, even though I never thought of him that way while growing up.

My dad faced plenty of risks every time he pushed off from the dock. But he knew how to reach the honey hole where the fish were, get them on board, process them, return home safely, and get them sold so he could continue to support his family and better our lives.

Similarly, as an investor, your goal is to:

- Accumulate the assets you need by setting out on the financial seas,
- Plan appropriately to get where you need to go,
- And protect your bounty against the storms we know will hit so that it will afford you the life you want in retirement.

How might you handle all that? The answer is certainly not to give up or put your head in the sand and hope for the best. And it's sure not to push off the dock willy-nilly. You need to know where you're headed when it comes to investing, what to do when you get there, and how to get home safely despite any unexpected life events or financial storms.

The news abounds with advice about what you need to do to accomplish that. There's so much information out there that it can be tough to get past all the noise and focus on what's really important. That's where a financial captain comes in. Every valuable financial ship needs a captain. Like my dad, I help make sure that the boat you're going to set out to sea on is sturdy. Then I help people get to where they need to go and let them know when they've arrived.

That last bit isn't nearly as obvious as it sounds.

Nick, a 59-year-old engineer, loved his job until new managers stepped in. He mentioned how unhappy he had become at work when we got together to review his retirement planning. "I can live with the fact that I don't like them," he said of his new managers. "But I don't trust them."

Like everyone, he had a pie-in-the-sky number in his head of how much he'd need to retire. As a result, he figured that retiring immediately wasn't an option. That changed once we ran the mathematical computation and showed him that even if he and his wife, Mary, lived to 100, they'd still have plenty.

As you've probably figured out, I'm not in the theorizing business. I'm a financial planning business owner on the front lines, whose job is to create and protect retirees' nest eggs. Much of what we do day in and day out at Beauport Financial Services involves getting families ready for retirement through planning, managing their wealth, and protecting them against the downside risks we all face.

After having the privilege and responsibility of sitting in the pilothouse of clients' financial ships during the Great Recession of 2008 and then COVID in 2020, as well as many other economic storms preceding and following those recessions, one definite thing I've learned is that few people hire a captain for calm seas and easy sailing. It's when the wind is howling, the skies are dark, and the seas are rough that a captain is essential. Though nobody's physical life was in danger during the downturn that hit in 2008, these folks certainly had their entire financial lives at stake as they searched for a safe harbor in which to ride out the storm.

Providing guidance and game plans as the seas changed so swiftly has been and continues to be quite a journey. Still, never in a million years did I plan to be an author and write up what I've learned along the way. I blame the creation of this book on my father. So much of what I believe about investing came from watching him earn his living on the precarious sea.

This is *not* a book on how to get rich, which stocks to pick or to avoid, what fund to buy, which specific type of life insurance coverage or income annuity you need, or what financial solution is best for your portfolio. My aim is much greater than that. This is a book about how to accumulate, protect, and pass on meaningful assets for a defined purpose and to avoid losing them along the way, which is paramount. You'll learn how to best prepare for your silent business partners: cost of living rises and taxation. We'll talk about how you can weather the storms, otherwise known as recessions, by having a seaworthy and properly prepared ship able to change course when needed—one that's equipped with proper instrumentation and tools, along with a clear sailing plan that includes a port of safety.

While following a process to steady your financial ship in both calm and rough seas is a worthy, challenging pursuit, it's a downright critical one when the storms come, as they always do. Your finances—and the financial legacy you'll pass on to your family—are only as sound as your process. Once the process is identified and articulated, the strategic financial solutions become self-evident. A successful process establishes one of two things: whether or not you're ready as a pre-retiree to enter into financial independence with confidence or, if you're already retired, whether maintaining your course or setting a new one is prudent.

Our role at Beauport is to make sure you have the navigational chart you need to make those decisions and establish a course that provides what you need on the financial front.

What does swordfishing have to do with any of this? The connections between running a successful swordfishing business and creating a thriving retirement income practice are not as crazy as one might think. In fact, as you'll see, they're too obvious to avoid.

For starters, just like a sword captain, you must have the confidence to push off from the relative safety of the dock with a navigational plan in hand. Then you'll need to:

- Use your instruments.
- Put plans into action.
- Make assessments along the way to maximize opportunity, taking in data and information from others but relying upon your captain for a profitable and safe voyage and return.
- Monitor what is on board and what is expected from each day at sea.
- Alter course due to weather or volatility and adapt as necessary.
- Fish!
- Prep and process your catch.
- Steam home and take inventory, assessing the trip along with what changes to enact right away and what changes can wait.

Once safely back in port, you'll want to decide whether to stay the course or change direction as you consider the macro and microeconomic landscape.

With swordfishing, there's always the mystery of the deep blue sea and hunting for what is unseen beneath the surface. Drop a line, set a hook, and see what happens. Investing is much the same. In both cases, we don't need to know all the secrets that lie below. But we do need to know what we are fishing for, where to fish, why we are fishing at all, and how to get back home.

Retiring is serious business, and being financially independent is a big deal. No wonder the decisions are difficult—this is new territory for you both in terms of finances and lifestyle. I'm willing to bet this is the first time you've entered such uncharted and unfamiliar waters. How many times in your life have you ever attempted something meaningful for the very first time and wound up with a perfect outcome? In all likelihood, never, unless you got lucky once or twice. That's not something you can afford to count on during this most important—and final—financial voyage of your life.

The ocean is as daunting to many as the idea of preparing for retirement. Although there are mountains of information on how to save, what to invest in, and where to put your money, our financial literacy is low, while our emotions surrounding money are usually high. That's just as lethal a combination as a shortage of knowledge and skill mixed with super-charged emotion would be on a boat like the Andrea Gail. And we know all too well what happened there.

So, let's raise our financial savvy. The forthcoming stories and chapters in this practical book are intended to be an everlasting tribute to the lessons my dad provided, unknowingly perhaps, and a compass for navigating both the crests and the troughs of the financial seas. Step aboard!

CHAPTER 1

DISCOVERING YOUR WHY? ASSETS WITH A PURPOSE

The North Atlantic winds lashed front, back, and sideways across a violent sea, crashing against every square foot of stainless steel and triple-reinforced marine glass the boat possessed. The chain links attached to the outriggers clamoring against the 100-pound steel pole had rendered conversation inside the pilothouse impossible, even if there had been someone there to talk to. Captain Charlie was alone, as he had been for the better part of the previous three days, chain-smoking cigarettes and pounding caffeine from endless pots of coffee as he struggled to keep the bow straight into the towering greenish-gray waves. Up they went, climbing the equivalent of a three-story building only to plummet back down and rise again and again and again.

The Andrea Gail and its crew of five experienced, grizzled longliners (called that because they routinely handled up to 40 miles of fishing line) had already been out swordfishing for three weeks in the late summer of 1989. The 17,000 pounds of prized North Atlantic swordfish in the hold, packed neatly on ice to protect the meat and keep it as fresh as possible, testified to a productive trip. With just the right amount of diesel fuel left, Captain Charlie, who only eight years before had traded steady fish warehouse work for the risky yet potentially lucrative work of swordfishing, had opted to turn back toward his home port of Gloucester, Massachusetts.

Dad, already a father of three at the young age of 20, didn't dream of being a swordfisherman, let alone a sword captain. But he was very determined to give his children a better opportunity and quality of life than his eighth-grade education had afforded him. He had said he would take my brother and me commercial fishing just once to make sure we would never romanticize the potentially lucrative occupation, but he never did. My brother and I didn't hold him to that promise (or was it a threat?). We already knew that fishing was damn hard, dangerous work.

"Derek, you will earn a better living with your head than with these," he told me repeatedly, always showing me his thick, calloused hands. "You and your two siblings are going to college. Period."

He was determined to do his part when it came to financing our higher education. A dead-end, low-skill job wasn't going to get that done. Friends of Dad's whom he respected were taking the chance and heading out of Gloucester Harbor for weeks at a time to longline swordfish in hopes of significant compensation. He decided to do the same. With a wife and three young kids, giving up a steady paycheck was undoubtedly a risky move. Effort did not always equate to fish in the hold of the boat. No fish landed after much toil meant no wages. Pretty simple and basic. Being in the right spot with lots of swords on the line and the first haul back into port—bingo! Ultimately, the potential to earn more at sea than with his dryland job, to be part of a seasoned crew and boat, and to learn the ins and outs of the swordfishing business on the North Atlantic sounded just too promising to pass up. In 1980, at age 25, Dad chose commercial fishing as his new profession, with an eye to ultimately being the boss and running his own ship. Four years later, in 1984, he took over the helm of the Andrea Gail, which he would captain for five years.

He had been hooked after his first swordfishing trip on the fiberglass-hulled boat Linnea C. During that maiden voyage to the Grand Banks, in addition to swordfish, he saw dolphins, dolphinfish (also known as mahi-mahi), tuna, and whales. This was more than just a fishing trip; it was an adventure, and they made good money, too.

Now, nine years since that first swordfishing trip as a greenhorn, he would need all that experience and then some to get himself, the crew, and the catch back to port safely.

They had turned for home as soon as all the huge fish they had caught had been secured. As usual, the crew had done what they could to ready the vessel for the next outing, all the while dreaming about what the price at the dock would be for their bounty upon their return.

Two days into the steam home, Hurricane Gabrielle violently greeted them on the course Captain Charlie had charted for Gloucester. He knew the storm was coming north from the Carolinas and figured they would miss the brunt of it as it passed by ahead of him by hundreds of miles and finally dissipated. But the storm stalled along the coast of Nova Scotia, putting the Andrea Gail smack in the middle of its path. They couldn't run away from the storm. Traveling only 10 knots a day instead of 100-plus has a way of consuming the precious and limited fuel reserved for the trip home, and most of the 20,000 gallons had already been used during the trip out and the harvest. Besides, as a seasoned captain, Dad knew full well that he had to head right into the teeth of the storm so that the 72-foot-long boat with its 20-foot beam would ride up and down the crests and troughs of the waves, not allowing the storm to run into the stern and overtake the open area working deck.

With no option except to stay on the carefully plotted course, Captain Charlie fought the wheel of the Andrea Gail. His stomach churned with every 30-foot drop as if on an endless roller coaster. Seas that huge have a way of getting and keeping your constant attention, regardless of how safe, big, and durable you think your 100-ton steel vessel is.

As the tropical storm-force winds attempted to whip the boat this way and that, the chances of the vessel making it safely home lay solely in the hands of its skilled captain. The autopilot setting is of no use in a storm—it doesn't react fast enough. The radar is sporadic and equally useless—repeated 30-foot waves spraying whitewash across both the stern and bow of the ship create too much interference and can prompt false readings.

Captain Charlie stared out at the heavy, dark seas, illuminated only by the deck light, which also captured the boat's proud U.S. flag ripping straight sideways in the constant 70-knot wind. Desperate to keep the Andrea Gail pointed in the right direction so they could reach port before running out of fuel, he prayed that the two eight-cylinder diesel engines wouldn't fail. Without those, he knew they'd be toast—a powerless, rudderless vessel amid this nasty storm would be a death sentence for the boat and potentially the crew. The last thing he wanted was to have to make that dreaded *may-day, may-day* call for help, a call that very possibly couldn't be answered.

As the chain links attached to the outriggers clamored against the 100-pound steel pole, providing a constant audible reminder of the tempest, the crew, as tense as their captain, did what they could, but that wasn't much. Captain Charlie slept very little during the 12 days it took to get home, the anxiety as evident in his bloodshot eyes as in his taut body and raspy voice. When he couldn't fight the need to shut his eyes, experienced Marvin Wilson—the 56-year-old Mr.-Fix-It engineer and the most trustworthy and seasoned man on the boat—would spell Dad. But those compulsory naps never lasted very long.

Captain Charlie knew they were in for it. The radar, when it worked, showed no sign of the storm letting up anytime soon. The only comfort lay in knowing that Frank W. "Billy" Tyne Jr., his friend and at the time the swordfishing captain of the Haddit, was less than a mile off his port side. The Haddit was nowhere to be seen, of course, but the two consistently checked in with each other as they kept an eye on the fuel reserves and general boat conditions, comforted by the fact that they were close by each other should something go terribly wrong.

Captain Charlie did make it home safely. So did Billy Tyne, who would not be so lucky a few years later after taking over captaining the Andrea Gail when my dad finally hung up his swordfishing oilskins. But Hurricane Gabrielle had given Dad the jitters once and for all. He'd already had to don a survival suit and be plucked out of the Atlantic waters by the Coast Guard after a boat he was on had sunk, and he didn't want to push his luck swordfishing anymore.

Captain Charlie holding a cod on the deck of the Josephine, a Gloucester dragger, during his post-swordfishing days.

Mom had been pressing that very point for some time. "Time to stop swordfishing, Charlie, and do something else," she had repeated after the last few trips to the Grand Banks. This time he listened. With a newfound respect for the seas and Mother Nature—and maybe just a little more confidence in the boat, the crew, and even himself—he finished out the swordfishing season with two more trips in September and October. Then, convinced that he could ply his craft under less ridiculous working conditions and make a safer buck ground fishing, he made the switch.

Dragging for cod, haddock, and flounder would entail calmer seas and a much shorter commute, which meant less time on the ocean and more time at home to see his family. Besides, he sensed that the swordfish he had been after would soon be classified as an endangered North Atlantic species. He knew American-zoned water stocks were no longer as plentiful as they had been in the early '80s, which meant more time and effort at sea and less profit at the dock. It was time to alter course and get out.

In fishing, nothing can be taken for granted. A couple of years after luck or premonition guided Dad to trade swordfishing for ground fishing, the historically tragic perfect storm hit the Northeast. The confluence of three substantial weather systems in 1991—a Nor'easter with extremely high winds, a low-pressure area ripe for storms coming east from the central part of the U.S., and a hurricane coming up from Florida—created a nasty party in the Atlantic. The waves were crazy, with at least one reaching a height of close to 100 feet from trough to crest, the highest ever recorded. The Andrea Gail, which had headed toward the waters off Nova Scotia for one last fishing run before the season's end, was nowhere near land when the wild sea that gobbled up hundreds of New England homes and businesses hit. The boat sank on its way home, and all on board were lost, including Dad's friend Billy Tyne.

No one, Dad included, knows what actually happened during that storm. But every swordfishing captain knows the dangers of the trade.

So why run the risk of fishing at all? Dad's answer was simple: opportunity.

That's precisely why we invest.

The Taste of a Good Trip
I didn't exactly grow up poor. After a bad swordfishing trip, a "broker," our family would eat tuna casseroles and lots of pasta for a month or so, or have pancake dinners more frequently until the next anticipated healthy paycheck. On the flip side, we celebrated a good trip by going out to dinner. The Millstone restaurant in Ipswich, Massachusetts was one of my folks' favorites. My mom, a teetotaler usually, would enjoy a White Russian, Dad, a Cape Codder along with the steak he'd always order and that deliciously baked oatmeal molasses bread slathered in freshly whipped butter. I always got stuffed chicken or prime rib and soda.

Those outings were the exception rather than the rule because we certainly didn't have a lot of extra money even with Dad's new gig as a swordfisherman. Overall, the new trade was financially rewarding, but there wasn't ever much left over with three growing kids, rent, car payments, health care, insurance, and retirement to consider, as there were no benefits provided by the boat. When a family friend would take my brother and me to wrestling events or games at the Boston Garden, we wouldn't ask Mom for spending money before leaving, knowing she did not have any to give us. Once there, we were too proud to ask for a drink or snack, so we just went without.

I've never forgotten that feeling of not having enough to buy what I wanted. I first learned that lesson as a young boy. When I was 12, on a Saturday summer afternoon, my friends decided they were going to the arcade to play video games. I ran home to ask Dad for some money so I could grab lunch and play games with my buddies. I raced up the dark, wood-paneled stairs of our apartment into the kitchen and told my folks I was heading downtown with my friends.

"Fine," they said after asking me who I would be with.

"Can I have some money?" I asked.

My dad reached into the right pocket of his blue jeans with those stubby, weathered fingers and handed me one wrinkled, folded dollar bill.

"That's all I got," he said.

I remember this whole short interaction as if it happened today. I also remember, to my chagrin, that I couldn't hide my disappointment as I looked down at that dollar, knowing it wouldn't get me a snack or lunch, and would only buy me five tokens for video games. That translated into about 15 minutes of arcade pleasure since I hadn't much practice and wasn't very good.

I spent the better part of that afternoon watching my friend, Joe, and some other buddies snack on vending machine treats and play video games long after I was done. After that, I started helping Joe on his paper route, then treated myself to day-old doughnuts for a dime at the Maplewood Sweet Shop or spent the small amount he shared with me on candy. The following summer, I wanted my own pocket money, so at 13, I got my first real job, dishwashing at The Gull Restaurant for minimum wage. It was honest and hard work, and now I could save my own spending money and not subject my friends or my loving parents to looks of discontent.

At that time, money afforded me fun, kid experiences, and the freedom to jump on my bicycle and head to the candy store and the arcade whenever I wanted. As an adult, I have figured out the difference between wanting and needing something. But I'm determined never to have that sense of not having enough again.

Making sure you have enough money also explains why you need to invest. Sure, investing can be just as risky as swordfishing, since the financial seas can be as rough as the seas that swallowed the Andrea Gail. The perfect economic storm of 2008 taught us that. Still, most of us need a financial solution.

The fact is that if you want to retire, you have to get serious about saving—and the sooner, the better—if you don't want to outlive your assets. As you already know all too well, you can no longer lean on a pension, since those are basically a thing of the past. Add to this lack of secure income during the jubilee years and the fact that many of you are part of a sandwich generation squeezed between the price of your kids' education and the cost of taking care of aging parents as they decline in health and require nursing homes, medical care facilities, or home renovations to accommodate physical needs or home care.

With all these demands and our increasing longevity, it's crazy not to be saving for a retirement that's going to last almost as long as your working life. But that's become the norm. Most people in this country who are in a 401k plan have just over $134,000 saved for retirement, according to a 2024 Nerd Wallet report. If they've invested at all, it's to avoid the tax bite and the inflation hit. While some have a vague notion of what their life will be like during retirement, a 2019 CNBC article states that a staggering 90 percent of Americans are scared of even talking to a financial advisor. That's almost as crazy as how little they've saved since a financial advisor's mission is to help you get where you want to go monetarily.

Sure, saving money is going to hurt a little. Just putting $15,000 a year into SEP IRA to get a tax break requires a sacrifice. That money could have allowed you to go to Italy for two months or to buy that trailer you've wanted. On the other hand, you put your kids through college to secure a better tomorrow for them. A lot of better tomorrows. Don't you owe yourself the same thing?

Of course, if you thought that your kids' college education was expensive, you're not going to believe how much it will cost you to live out all those golden years in the way to which you have—or would like—to become accustomed. So, it's critical to start saving as early and often as possible. If you wait to save and invest until you have so much money that you won't feel the sting, it will be too late.

Still, those of you who have delayed taking the plunge on investing—or even saving—can take heart. In dealing with money and investing, most mistakes can be corrected once they've been identified. Since we're usually not talking about health and safety or life-and-limb circumstances, guidance can be pursued at any point in time.

Enjoying financial success and long-term income stability is seldom about picking the correct stock to purchase or turning in the winning lottery ticket. It has so much more to do with building good habits early on, repeating them consistently, and making sure your outflow is never more than your inflow. Tucking away for your future 10 to 15 percent of what you earn takes discipline. Attaching meaning to the money you're investing will get you through the tougher times once you've developed your saving routine. But that's easier said than done.

We are creatures of habit with formed behaviors and entrenched reactions to money. Breaking those spending habits and developing new saving practices isn't going to be easy. Heck, if it was effortless, then everyone could do it painlessly, and we'd all wake up in our 60s as multimillionaires. That's why you have to start now, today, no matter how old—or young—you are. Whatever your financial condition, you'll want to save just enough each month to make it hurt a little. By sacrificing a bit on a consistent basis, and monitoring the growth of your retirement nest egg, your spending habits will be hardwired by the time you successfully retire. Even if you can afford to splurge nightly on expensive first-growth Bordeaux with dinner, you won't because it just won't feel right.

Great spending habits are hard to break. So are the nasty ones. That's why you have to have a vision as well as a plan. Otherwise, it's going to be near impossible to maintain that consistent financial sacrifice called saving for retirement.

Money with Purpose
Any successful financial plan has a stated purpose and defined goal just as any fruitful swordfish trip has a navigational plan and built-in contingencies. The *why* component of personal financial and retirement planning is just as paramount as *what* to do with your accumulated nest egg and *how* to put it to best use.

The *why* in fishing is pretty clear. You want to find fish, catch fish, get home safely, and turn that fish into treasure. The *why* related to targeted financial planning for a successful retirement could be characterized as simple, too, I suppose. You want to earn money, diligently save some of that money, invest well, and create an income stream—or treasure—from said abundance for your retirement. Anything left over goes to the next generation or charity, and life is good. Right?

That's my *why*. Since why you set sail is as important as what you're fishing for, you need to determine your reason. That makes all the difference, since *what* you invest in and *how* you do it is insignificant compared to *why* you do it.

What's your *why*?

Investing in something meaningful to you rather than merely avoiding taxes or the impact of inflation gives purpose to your financial sacrifice. Sometimes, that *why* behind a desired outcome is obvious. Maybe it has to do with your physical and mental health, or your family and/or spouse's well-being. Maybe you're investing with an eye to business, vocational, or educational opportunities. Or maybe your faith, your community, a hobby, or a cause compels you to make that financial move. Other times, however, your *why* is buried so deep inside you that you don't even know it's there.

It's time to dig out that answer. My job is to help you do that.

Your answer is what gets you up in the morning and drives you forward. It's also what keeps you on your financial course and reminds you of your greater purpose when the financial waters get turbulent, and the skies are dark.

Once we ferret out that deep-seated *why*, we can determine how to strategically and purposefully deploy your hard-earned assets in a way that will enrich your life as well as your legacy and fulfill your clearly defined vision. To do that, I'll ask you questions like:

- What does money mean to you?
- What do you treasure?
- What is it about money that's important to you?
- What privileges, opportunities, and options does money afford you?

- Would you rather have unlimited time or unlimited financial resources?
- Why and what would you do with all your time or all the money?
- When is enough, enough?
- What are your goals?
- What do you dream of doing someday? This is important, since your assets, once they've accumulated, can afford you tremendous opportunity.

Every financial advisor has their own way of approaching these issues. You want to find a professional with the passion and the prowess to advise on money issues and advocate for you in the financial marketplace, while effectively helping you complete your life voyage.

That's why I love being a financial advisor. I knew that's what I wanted to do the day I heard banker John Fleming speak to my junior high social studies class on career day. Like my dad, I want to help my clients bring home the catch on the good fishing days and get them safely through any storms that arise while they're still working, as well as the imperfect storm of retirement. And I want to help them chart a course that reflects the larger and ultimately most important questions related to their money.

Once we've determined what drives your investments, we'll:

- Discuss what your investments are destined for.
- Evaluate what you're currently doing, what's working, the timeline, what you need to live fruitfully during your last

20 to 30 years, and how the money measures up against inflation and financial risks.
- Ascertain what changes we would make and create a plan that addresses all potential risks.
- Help you reach your long-term goals.

My job as the captain is to make sure you can enjoy the scenery for the rest of your life. So, in addition to planning for the future, I'll also give you a financial reality check along the way. I'll essentially tell you, "This is what we have on board. We know we're going to be sailing for a while and that the vessel needs to be maintained."

In five years, if you want to buy a condo on a tropical island, I'm going to take inventory, just like a captain monitoring how much fish is in the hold and whether it's time to return to shore. If we're on schedule with your investable net worth (not including your home or art collection), I'll give you a thumbs up. If not, I'll say, "I wouldn't suggest that right now. We're a little behind schedule." You can't make those kinds of educated decisions if you don't know where you're at, where you need to go, and what kind of a boat you're in.

I want to be clear here. As much as we'd like to, financial advisors like me can't help everyone. If you only have an eight-foot dinghy, you're not going to the Grand Banks. There's only so much you can do with a tiny boat. But we can definitely help you trade up so that you wind up in the kind of vessel that can keep you afloat no matter what the conditions.

Do you need a financial planner? Despite the surge of new robo-advisor models, planning and investing for a lifetime of income are not optimally performed with the Home Depot do-it-yourself approach. You obviously don't operate on yourself or fill your own cavities. Finding the right expert is just as important when it comes to your money because that's what will set you up for your retirement.

All too often, people think about retiring *from* a job or a career rather than retiring *to* something else. Just as my dad knew there was a bigger and better opportunity ahead for me, your retirement can lead to something bigger and better in your life. You just have to have the means to get there. When you push off the dock and embark on this new voyage, you need to know the financial risks have already been navigated and that you have the best chance to meet your living needs and your giving needs, and to achieve your goals for this next phase of your life. That means hiring the right captain. That's next.

CATCH OF THE DAY:

- Discipline today will bear fruit later on. When your assets hold great meaning and purpose, it's so much easier to remain disciplined and build good financial habits.
- Ships are designed to be sailed, on purpose, with purpose. Financial assets are intended to be utilized with purpose, too, according to a desired goal and outcome. Your financial ship shouldn't stay dry at the dock. Launch it with a purpose and destination in mind. Answering your question of *why* is a great place to start. If you care to have a fantastic, final stage of your financial life, then knowing what you want and why makes that last great financial journey all the more meaningful.
- Algorithms do not understand your financial hopes and dreams, nor does a non-emotional computer model. Seek out a financial planner with whom you can share your innermost thoughts and communicate your *why*. Aligning your financial vision with the process and planning employed on your behalf—that's where the magic happens.

CHAPTER 2
EVERY FINANCIAL SHIP NEEDS A CAPTAIN— CHOOSING YOURS

Let's assume you're ready to retire, and you have two million dollars in your retirement accounts. That might sound impossible to some of you and low to others, but just play along—we'll be talking about accumulating wealth later in the book. But back to my hypothetical situation. Since you're no longer going to be earning income, you've determined that you need to replace $100,000 per year with your portfolio income, in the form of dividends, interest, and appreciation.

Why bother with hiring a financial advisor at all?

The answer is simple. Let's say you're one of those success stories. You've got enough money every month, and your assets are protected, at least as far as you know. You think you've got it all figured out. But we don't know what we don't know. And unless you're a certified financial planner, if you're handling your own investments you're likely missing out on opportunities and not considering all the financial protection checks and balances that are so vital when it comes to protecting your nest egg. That's why you need to bring in an expert.

At Beauport Financial, for example, we comprehensively take care of the whole financial picture. We design a game plan for how to get you where you need to be financially in the accumulation phase and then how to best position those assets to maintain your desired lifestyle into and through retirement. All that starts with a conversation so that we get clear about what's important to you and you get clear on what we offer.

A financial planner must provide you with a well-defined value proposition based on an assessment of your goals and needs. Of course, financial planning, like commercial fishing, can be a risky business. How you and your financial advisor address those risks, which we'll talk about a lot more in Chapter 3, will determine your financial success or failure, so that has to be factored in as well.

Risky Business

Essentially, there are three ways you can handle financial risk. You can:

- Avoid it,
- Manage it,
- Transfer it.

You want your captain to speak to how they deal with investment-related risk. Solid planners and competent financial captains don't just promise terrific returns; they focus with intention and purpose on all three approaches to handling risk. On the other hand, financial ships were meant to be sailed, and pushing off the dock always involves some element of risk. So, while we'll discuss keeping a certain amount of cash on hand to make sure you have a safety net and can ride out the average financial storms, the idea here is to do whatever you can to minimize that risk vis-a-vis what the market can bear as you set out on those perilous financial seas.

This sure doesn't mean going at it alone.

It turns out that many people left to their own devices and instinctual behavior usually do the wrong thing financially when it comes to managing financial risk. Study after study comparing investor behavior and returns with the financial markets' performance demonstrates this. The Dalbar study, which looked at investor results over a period of 20 years, showed that while the index rose 9.85 percent, the average investor made only 5.19 percent.

The reason for this regrettable trend is simple—we're human and we're emotional.

Instead of charting a course and trusting a competent captain, too many of us repeatedly buy shares when feeling overconfident and sell shares when market conditions look or feel ominous. In short, instead of buying low and selling high, that well-known recipe for financial success, we do the opposite.

This tendency isn't our fault—we're wired this way. It's not easy to ride into a storm when running away from it feels like the right thing to do. But the decisions we make at financially significant moments such as retirement, divorce, inheritance, stock distribution, pension rollout, or the sale of a business or property—or during economically stressful times such as recessions—have a long-term impact on our finances. And while we all blow it from time to time, those blunders when it comes to our money can be downright disastrous, especially if you are near, or in, retirement.

Once you've retired, every 1 to 2 percent mistake you make related to an investment, tax, or allocation decision represents many thousands of dollars of financial pain. During the accumulation phase, when you have fewer assets and are still working, you can usually make amends. If a swordfishing boat realizes that the ice machine needed to keep the fish fresh has malfunctioned on the first day of fishing, there's time to fix it before too much of the catch has been lost. That same problem, when 20,000 pounds of fish are in the hold with no fresh ice to keep the catch cold and the boat still two weeks from home, represents a whole different scale of loss.

In short, you need a comprehensive game plan, and it's not going to be the same one that guided your pre-retirement financial decisions. Barbara and Geoff realized that when their estate planning attorney referred them to me. At the time, Geoff, then in his late 60s, had just sold his dentistry practice.

"Do you have any kind of coordinated game plan for what's next?" asked his estate planning attorney.

"No," replied Geoff. "I'm talking to my accountant. I'm talking to my insurance broker. I'm talking to the 401k broker regarding my 401k plan from work. Then I've got these investment accounts, so I'm talking to the investment person. Plus, I've got $150,000 in the bank in cash, so I'm consulting with my banker as well."

"Geez," the attorney said. "You should talk to a retirement planner, someone who specializes in retirement income planning." Then he gave Geoff and Barbara my name and number.

As I found out the day I went to the couple's house to meet them, not only were the five professionals Geoff was consulting not working in concert with each other, they didn't even know each other. By the end of our conversation, during which I shared a two-minute video called "The Retirement Income Survival Kit" about financial risks, and another short video about what we, at Beauport, do for our clients, Geoff and Barbara realized that while they'd clearly had a game plan related to accumulating their money, they now needed a very different income plan for retirement.

You must make the right decisions when it comes to your money. You've spent years saving and investing it, and now you've arrived at your waypoint, Dad's fishing term for your destination. But do you know how to correctly answer questions like:

- Can I retire comfortably now or wait another few years?
- When do I start investing and into what?
- How much can I spend and for how long?
- What risks do I need to address?
- Do I take the pension or roll the money out of the qualified plan?
- Do I take the lump-sum inherited asset or periodically distribute it?
- Should I tap into the tax-free savings this year or leverage the taxable funds based on my tax situation?
- How long is my money going to last?

Even though we're not exactly talking about troubled waters with the above questions, if you're not a financial planner, I'm guessing you only have a vague idea, at best, about how to respond. So why wouldn't you want a competent captain in your financial planning wheelhouse to manage all those money-related considerations? With a good captain and a prudent plan (which we'll talk about in the next chapter), you won't have to abandon ship during a financial storm. Instead, you'll know how you're going to ride it out.

Unfortunately, few people hire a captain during calm seas and smooth sailing. They wait until the wind rages, the skies are black, the seas are treacherous, and vital investment decisions need to be made. That makes as much sense as hiring an architect after your house crumbles. In construction, an architect and a builder team up to erect a house that will hopefully withstand whatever Mother Nature decides to throw its way. When it comes to investing and having a great journey in retirement, a financial captain designs a game plan ahead of time, knowing that you want to protect your assets during the imperfect financial storms or recessions that, as we've already established, have hit on average every six-and-a-half years since World War II, according to a history.com report. These recessions tend to last about 10 months and are characterized by a significant decline in the country's gross domestic product (GDP) for two consecutive quarters. They aren't to be confused with market corrections, defined as relatively short-lived 10 percent drops in the market that occur almost every year. Just as in fishing, these course corrections, which typically last from a week to a month or two, happen consistently. The good news is that 75 percent of the time, we end up positive for the year. That other 25 percent of the time is why we have to focus on safeguarding your financial resources and/or have the foresight to buy additional shares while prices are low.

I wish more people did that. It would spare them so much angst and pain.

From early 2008 to early 2009, right in the eye of the financial storm later dubbed the "Great Recession" here in the U.S., Beauport Financial had one of its best years ever for asset growth as shaken investors looking for reassurance came calling. With dire forecasts and no end in sight, many—especially those in or near retirement—wanted to have a personal conversation relevant to their situation and needed immediate help figuring out what to do.

Of course, they were aware that they hadn't hired a financial captain to steer their ship, but they didn't understand until it was too late just how much risk they had taken on. All they knew about their assets was that they had accounts with names and numbers on them, and the numbers were going down each quarter. It fell on us to help them safeguard what they could, and to help them determine what to do about the damage inflicted on their financial well-being and their legacy. The irony is that had they gone into the storm prepared and then ridden it out, they would not only have recouped their losses; over time they would have significantly increased their asset base. At the start of the next chapter, you'll read about one couple who jumped ship instead of riding it out, a decision they likely wouldn't have made if they'd had a financial plan in place and a pro to oversee it.

Every financial plan needs a financial planner just as every ship needs a captain. What happens when there is no financial game plan being carried out by a planner? Human emotions rule, and significant mistakes are made. Managing our human instincts and reactions to storms is just as essential when it comes to personal financial planning as it is on a swordfishing boat.

One of the world's best stock pickers and mutual fund managers, Fidelity Magellan manager Peter Lynch, earned 29+ percent annually during his tenure from 1977-1990. In his prime, one out of every ten Americans owned his Magellan Fund. Most of the investors in his managed mutual fund, however, saw one-fifth of that return. Those were the lucky ones. Others lost money. How is this possible? Because during the inevitable lows, instead of resolving to trust the process of one of best stock pickers ever, the average Joe sold his shares based on news of the markets going down, often buying them back later at much higher prices.

It's hard to think clearly and make good money decisions under duress and confusion, and it's really easy to make knee-jerk decisions when things look grim. A competent captain can recognize the difference between a normal course correction due to a lousy quarter or month or some bad news as opposed to a more serious downturn. That's why good financial captains (otherwise known as fiduciaries) can be relied upon to provide a sense of calm and clarity or to alter course and implement changes needed to weather the storm.

The same applies to swordfishing captains. Part of Dad's success lay in realizing that the seas can be treacherous and downright fickle and that sometimes all the skill a captain possesses is required just to save what they can. That comes from not overreacting, while still knowing when to batten down the hatches when it's going to get rough.

Think back to the story in the last chapter, where Dad was faced with that whopper of a storm and a rapidly diminishing amount of fuel. He had to figure out how to mitigate the crisis. He knew he could head for a safe port in Canada where he would seek to unload the catch, but that could have jeopardized the crew's potential profit by extending the trip and adding to the total expenses. That's assuming he could offload the fish at all. Or he could press on into the storm, with just enough fuel left to get them within spitting distance of home base in Gloucester Harbor. With the help of a fellow fisherman who towed them in the last few miles, they made it safely to the dock and cashed in. Dad's carefully calculated risk had paid off.

This is where great and experienced captains earn their keep, right?

Of course, successful swordfishing and financial captains alike need to know how to land the fish in the first place—otherwise, there's nothing to keep safe or manage.

Dad knew everything there was to know about the art and science of swordfishing. He knew, for example, that the Atlantic swordfish, which can grow up to many hundreds of pounds and live for several decades, has a unique tissue in its brain that allows it to swim at depths of hundreds of feet or tens of feet based upon the most opportune place in the current. Not just a cold-water or warm-water fish, the swordfish can adapt to the current, weather, feeding, and environmental conditions, thereby increasing its odds for survival. Dad also knew that the swordfish uses its big, dark eyes to hunt, which is why fishermen set the lines and bait hooks using the full moon calendar. Squid, which swordfish feed on, rise toward—and concentrate around—the ceiling formed by the reflected moonlight. That draws the swordfish.

The swordfish can't help themselves. Just as we humans are wired to want to stop fishing when the headlines are bad and later pounce on whatever is bright and shiny, swordfish are wired to go for the bait that's illuminated by the full moon and/or glow sticks.

For Dad, the science of swordfishing was obvious. Be aware of the ideal temperature of the water, time of year when the fish are prevalent, and have the right gear and bait ready to go on the cycle of the full moon. Of course, all the other worthy swordfishing captains in the area knew this as well. To be able to execute his game plan and go for the best spot where the water was, ideally, 67 to 69 degrees, Dad knew he had to beat the others to the expected fish hole. If you wound up being the last to show up, you not only had to avoid other vessels and gear, where you fished would be dictated by those in front of you. Inevitably, that meant fishing in colder waters potentially just outside the Gulf Stream current where you would catch lots of sharks (which are a lot less profitable than swordfish) since that's where sharks feed.

This is where the art of swordfishing comes in. Getting positioned with the boat and gear is just the start. You also have to time the setting and retrieval of the equipment and know when to cut your losses in order to fish more effectively another day.

Dad's expertise in both the science and the art of swordfishing resulted in him being one of the area's most successful swordfishing captains. That's the kind of captain you want skippering your boat—one who maintains a good crew, takes care of the vessel, and puts the boat on the fish.

On the financial front, you also want to put your money in the hands of an expert who knows not only how to land the kind of financial returns you're fishing for without exposing you to undue risk, but how to mitigate a financial crisis and then get back in the game. In short, you need a competent, caring captain and crew to navigate the ever-changing currents, times, and conditions along your retirement voyage.

A sound financial captain can help ensure you're fully prepared for life's investment journey by making sure that your investment strategy is sound and being attended to. As your financial ship motors over the crests of the wave as well as through the troughs, the captain monitors progress and changes course along the way, all while taking inventory and maintaining the ship. The objective is to do everything possible to make the journey home safe and predictable, so you know what you have for assets when you unload the catch since that's just as important as reeling in those assets in the first place. Dad would never have made it home safely in good weather or bad if he hadn't calculated the amount of fuel it takes to get home from the Grand Banks with approximately 25,000 pounds of swordfish in the hold.

I'd argue that too much of the financial industry has been focused on the accumulation side of assets, rather than what to do strategically with your treasure as you sail into retirement. You can't afford to spend all your time, energy, and focus on fishing only to realize there's only enough fuel to get you halfway home.

These days too many people seem to think they can cast their nets in retirement the same way they were fishing before retiring. Meanwhile, many know way too little about who is at the helm of their financial ship, assuming someone's there at all. The fact is that anyone with a boat, gear, and bait can catch fish when the fish are right under you, and the conditions are beautiful. But what do you do when they're not? Swordfishing is not a recreational sport, and neither is retirement planning.

No commercial fishing for me. It's all about being on the water and having fun when I'm not captaining my clients' financial ships.

So let me ask you. Who is the captain of your financial ship? And are they considering opportunities and risks you may not even know about?

Before you answer, let's consider two other questions:

1. What are you fishing for?
2. What business is your captain in?

Even the most seasoned and strategic captain can't deliver if they're fishing for something you don't want to catch. That's why you don't hire a shrimper, a tuna fisherman, or a ground fisherman to run your swordfishing operation. Similarly, if you're looking to accumulate and manage resources for retirement, you want to make sure you hire a financial planner who is qualified to do that. There are plenty of professionals in the financial arena with plenty of titles, including *stockbroker, manager of investment portfolios, life insurance broker, fee-only planner, income planner, long-term care specialist*, etc. They all handle a slice of the pie. But devising income plans for retirees isn't their niche. Only by looking at their qualifications do you know if they're the right captain with all the expertise necessary to oversee your financial ship.

Most people hire a CPA to do their taxes. As opposed to a bookkeeper, a certified CPA has gone through a specific course load and has to report to a higher authority. So why would you settle for less when hiring a financial planner? Even then, all financial planners are not created equal. In my case, for example, after a comprehensive course of study, I sat for—and passed—a two-day Certified Financial Planner test. According to Safe Landing Financial, only 30 percent of financial advisors in the U.S. have earned that Certified Financial Planner® (CFP) designation.

That's not the only difference between financial advisors. Here's what to look for:

Independence

In fishing, the most successful captains head to where they know the fish are running. Discounting any weather warnings, that's the only thing that matters. If your financial advisor is part of a full-service brokerage or a bank, their options can be more limited since they must choose their investments from the company pool. That's why why at Beauport Financial, we're independents, some of us for more than 20 years. We act as fiduciaries, the highest legal duty of one party to another, which binds one to act ethically in the other's best interests.

Transparency

The investment strategy advisors recommend can also be impacted by how they're compensated. Certain investment products carry high commissions. If a financial planner recommends that their client invest in those commissioned products, they'll add to their bottom line. Unfortunately, this doesn't always mean that they're adding to their client's bottom line.

Clear expectations are critical whenever money is involved. Dad couldn't control the cost of fuel, food, or bait, but he could certainly ensure that whatever was needed for a successful trip was well thought out and carefully calculated. Everyone involved knew the financial breakdown, which

I'll explain in the next chapter, and how the system worked. Minimize the expenses with prudent management, catch the fish, and everybody wins.

I wish things were as clear in the financial planning world. We need to take the mystery out of what financial advisors do and how we get paid. You want to hire someone who can explain and demonstrate how they're compensated (we call that being transparent) so you know there's no conflict of interest. And let me remind you that you also want to work with a firm that champions you in the financial marketplace and sits on the same side of the table as you do.

Timing and Chemistry
Once you've established that you'll be working toward the same goal, you need to ascertain whether the person you're talking to is someone you'll feel comfortable opening up to. The fact is you're going to be discussing money, which often feels like a taboo subject. The right financial advisor will also ask you to share your hopes and dreams in order to make those part of your financial plan. That's why good chemistry is so critical.

Of course, the right timing is just as important. While planning for retirement can't start too early, perhaps you've put that off. Suddenly, one of those big life events hits. Maybe you decide to buy or sell a business. Maybe you decide to start a family. Maybe you suddenly inherit some money. No matter what the reason, you can no longer afford to sit on the sidelines. You need a game plan, which means finding the right financial advisor without delay.

Process

So now you know that you want to opt for a financial captain whom you can talk to and whose compensation lines up with your best interest. You also want to look for someone who can define in a couple of minutes how they would address your particular situation.

You want to ask:

What do you do for someone like me who has a couple million saved?

Or:

What do you do for someone like me who wants to save a couple million?

That's called achieving retirement clarity. You're looking for someone who can outline a game plan in one-, three-, and five-year segments.

Of course, you also want to look at performance. But if you're choosing your advisor simply based on the arbitrary performance of constructed portfolios, you're making a significant mistake. A boat owner doesn't hire someone to captain their ship based upon one good fishing trip that might simply be due to a lucky hit of a mother lode of fish. Successful captains like my dad depend on a proven, repeatable process and reliable tools. Dad didn't just look over the bow of his boat or at where all the other boats were headed when trying to find swordfish. He relied on his knowledge, his experience, and his radar.

Similarly, at Beauport, we lay out a repeatable, proven process for our clients. We look at your cash flow, your income plan, and your investment policy statement (IPS). The latter is your guide that tells you how you should be allocated, which we'll talk about more in the next couple of chapters. At the very least, that financial plan can prove reassuring, but in times of trouble, you'll know we've accounted for whatever imperfect financial storm your ship has to sail through. You won't need to jump into the lifeboats because of a lack of—or poor—planning.

Of course, continued success on the high seas also depends on a competent captain who brings along a seaworthy vessel and a caring—and cared-for—crew. That's why you want to look for someone with a reliable team.

Team
No one person can handle everything related to keeping your finances safe and in shipshape. Not even a trained professional. As a result, captains are only as good as the entire crew since they can't perform their duties if those on deck always need a hand or additional training. Financial planners rely on a team of experts—behind-the-scenes back-office support from trusted strategy specialists with expertise in everything from insurance and long-term care to income-generating annuities. This is also the peripheral team your planner leans on and communicates with when working with other professionals like a CPA or estate attorney to align your financial plan while taking into consideration your tax, legal, and economic opportunities. In short, you need to evaluate the crew as much as the captain.

When Dad was at sea for weeks at a time, without question nor hesitation, he trusted Billy Tyne. As an experienced captain himself, Billy had recommended Dad for his first big-time trip on a reputable swordfishing boat. He would ride out Hurricane Gabrielle with him, knew what needed to be done on a boat, and anticipated tasks and duties before others did.

When it came to anything related to mechanics, my dad trusted Marvin. He was a master at fixing any kind of equipment, ensuring that everything was operational before heading out to sea, and handling any maintenance issues while fishing. That part is critical since you can't fish with a dead engine, and you can't exactly call the repairman when you're days from home. Marvin was a genius in the engine room. Dad couldn't have made a move without the help of people like Billy and Marvin.

Similarly, we rely on the financial experts who are part of our team to help implement the strategy that our clients and we decide is the best plan. None of us goes it alone. But even the greatest captains with the world's best teams are a no-go if they don't realize that you are the most critical team member.

In addition to working on your behalf with the internal team, a good captain also needs to communicate externally with your other professional advisors. Whether you have an accountant, a state tax planning attorney, an estate planning attorney, an insurance agent, or whomever, everyone needs to be pulling in the same direction. If I don't know what your tax situation is, I can't possibly recommend investment strategies to help minimize the hit. Part of my role is to understand the full picture so I can make sure that all the advisors are working in your best interest.

Truth

Strong relationships matter since we will all be tested by the markets and economic conditions or, in my dad's case, by the less-than-predictable North Atlantic Ocean. In addition to needing someone competent in the pilothouse who can successfully bring home the catch and or safely get you through the storm, you need someone who will work with you to figure out the larger and ultimately most important questions related to your money. Even that's not enough. You need a captain who delivers the good news as well as the bad, in all types of weather, and doesn't hide when the seas are rough. In short, you want to find someone who will tell you the truth. Unless you know the full scoop—the good, the bad, and the ugly—you can't possibly make sound financial decisions.

Part of the deal I make with my clients is to tell it like it is, whether the news is positive or not, in a way that they'll understand. That's critical. Your planner must be able to speak your language. If you need color charts and pretty pictures to understand your projected cash flow or anything else, then you'd better find a planner who can provide that.

Ten Questions

I've already suggested a few ideas on what you might ask any financial planner you're considering. Here are ten more, which sum up a lot of what I've just talked about. You want to be sure to ask:

1. Whom do you serve, and what do you specialize in?
2. What business niche are you in? (Make sure that your financial advisor is fishing in the waters you care to be in and understands your needs.)
3. How do you advocate for your clients in the financial marketplace? (Will they fight for you, for example, to get the best life or disability insurance rate, to find the best income options for personal income annuities, or to keep fees and expenses down?)
4. Do you have a proven, repeatable process you can share with me?
5. Once we start working together, will you be able to outline a retirement game plan in multi-year segments?
6. Are you independent and acting as a fiduciary, or do you represent certain companies or financial institutions?
7. How are you compensated, and what is your fee structure? (Be clear on how your financial planner earns their fee to ensure there's no conflict of interest and that you understand the value proposition.)
8. Who is part of your team, and what is your process when it comes to your stated niche?
9. How and how often do you communicate with your clients?
10. How do you feel about sharing troubling news? (Having a reassuring captain who can give it to you straight and explain their reasoning about making—or not making—changes to your portfolio is essential.)

The Right Captain

Okay. By now, you have the basic idea down. You're looking for a Certified Financial Planner with a proven process. You know what questions you need to ask to figure out the rest.

But how do you launch your search for the right financial captain? Start by asking the other financial professional you're already working with, like your CPA or estate planning attorney, for recommendations.

You'll also want to find out from your financially successful friends or colleagues who they're working with and why. That might feel a bit awkward since we tend not to talk about money. But why? That tradition certainly isn't moving us forward. So, do ask around. It can save you time and help you make the right choice. When owner Bob Brown needed a captain for his swordfishing boat, he didn't interview a ton of people. Word on the street was that my dad, Captain Charlie Reed, was worth his salt. It was that simple.

What makes a sound captain? According to Dad, assuming basic competence, people skills, and a solid plan, the two key elements are:

1. Adaptability based on current and pending circumstances, which in my dad's world could mean the difference between life and death.
2. Sensing the needs of those around you.

The first relates to the management of the conditions you're presented with. A good captain assesses the goals of the client and their assets and then considers how and when to position those assets strategically in the financial marketplace. Knowing that the seas aren't always calm, the boat owner hires someone who has proven their ability to anticipate adverse conditions and do what's needed to keep both the boat and the crew safe and in good working condition.

The second is all about care meeting craft. It's not good enough to be competent. You have to care about everything and everyone. My dad taught me that. I remember him telling me about sensing that a newbie on his crew was mentally and physically tired. It had been a typically long, hard day of hauling back miles of line and hooks, dressing thousands of pounds of fish, stowing them correctly in the hold, then once again setting out those miles of line, baited hooks, and buoy markers before dinner. Instead of berating the new guy for lagging, Captain Charlie took over his work and sent him up to the pilothouse so he could take an extra break.

Of course, the owner wants the captain to put the boat on the fish. That's a given. But it's easy and misguided to focus just on the fish. A great crew on a lousy and inefficient boat can only do so much to harvest and protect the profits. A lousy crew on a sturdy, well-maintained, and state-of-the-art boat can also do significant damage to the harvest, costing everyone money and wasted effort to say nothing of all that frustration. That's why a vigilant captain knows what the people around him need and how to manage them, as well as how to maintain the ship.

Trust

In the end, it all boils down to trust. You need to be able to trust your captain to do what's right, even when you're not paying attention. You also need to be able to trust that your captain will do as much to protect your assets against the inevitable downturns as he or she does to acquire them.

I know all about trust because that one word defines my entire upbringing.

Dad was able to better himself and our family's financial situation as a swordfish captain because he earned the boat owner's trust.

Captain Charlie could leave for the better part of six months out of every year because he trusted Mom to hold down the fort. Upon return, Dad's routine was to unload fish, clean the boat, prep and stock it for the next trip, communicate orders to crew, and get back out to sea in a four- to five-day turnaround. April to October is a short season to make hay, roughly the same season as Major League Baseball. Still, these optimistic, ocean-hardened fishermen don't get signing bonuses or million-dollar financial contracts. Instead of guarantees, they face calculated risks as they chase and harvest something that nature provides via the warm, rhythmic currents of the Gulf Stream. No harvest equals no food to sell. Dad had plenty of concerns without worrying about us. He knew he didn't have to. Mom was rock solid on the home front.

My mom knew that everything had to be shipshape at home, or that would distract Dad from doing what he did best. So, in addition to her working a blue-collar job cutting and packing fish down on the wharf, she ran a tight ship at home. Not only did she handle all the household chores and maintenance, but she was also the bookkeeper, administrator, and logistical coordinator for Dad, both while he was at sea and when he was on dry land. She kept a maroon, spiral-bound notebook with all of Dad's takes from his trips. Since he was self-employed (at least according to the taxman), a chunk of each check had to be set aside for estimated taxes. She oversaw the household and the business expenses well, managing bank accounts for both savings and checking needs.

My parents talked once or twice a week while Dad was at sea, reviewing the mundane news about school and sports, as well as how the trip was going. Mom always had a good idea of what the paycheck would look like, which helped her figure out what bills to pay when.

Mom was the anchor at home while Dad was out at sea.

Of course, she also took care of her family. After each trip, she would clean a month's worth of his laundry and get him properly organized and prepped for another trip at sea. And while Dad was gone, she played the role of a loving yet stern mom. He trusted her to raise us right, and his trust was not misplaced.

Mom was the key to everything. She was the ballast when it came to us kids, getting us off to school, making sure the schoolwork was done, and managing everyone's extracurricular schedules. Breakfast was on the table in the morning, brown school lunch bags on the kitchen counter, and a hot family meal most nights, even if she had to stretch a dollar with groceries and meal prep when things got tight. More importantly, she helped create a family environment with an abundance of love, hugs, and verbal praise.

Little did I realize how much growing up in the home of a fisherman taught me about finance and active saving on a daily basis. In addition to taking care of us and the accounts, my frugal mom, who had quietly saved the money that enabled them to buy their first house, squirreled away money in the Christmas club, so there was cash to buy the mountain of toys that showed up under the tree every year.

She also wasn't shy when it came to encouraging us kids to make our own money. As a youngster, Mom would drive me to Good Harbor Beach at the end of a summer day. I would grab as many soda cans as I could from the overflowing barrels, put them in a large plastic bag, which I would drag along the sand to the next 55-gallon barrel. After she'd taken me to the local redemption center where I would recycle the cans for five cents apiece, we'd go back home, and I would count my dirty nickels, which I'd brought back in the garbage bag.

Only three years separated me, the oldest, from my youngest sibling, Charlie. Sister Tricia was in the middle. During the years that Dad chased swordfish across the North Atlantic, we were all certainly in our formative years, which I imagine, now that I'm a father, put extra stress and strain on Mom. She handled it all remarkably well. She set clear expectations right up front, so that we always knew where she stood and, in turn, where we stood. Dad had to do this with his crew, just as the boat owner had to do it with my dad before entrusting him with the Andrea Gail.

Mom could love, care, and show support, but she also told you when you were off course or plain ol' wrong. There could be no drama since that could create anxiety for Dad, who was already dealing with plenty of drama at sea. We were simply expected to do the right thing, be it with friends, at school, Sunday school, or in sports—no ifs, ands, or buts.

I was a teenager when I learned from my mom that sometimes deciding not to do something is as important as taking action. Early one August evening, when Dad was on a fishing trip, she overheard my friends chattering outside the open second-floor apartment windows as she was cleaning up from dinner. She knew we planned to go pool hopping that night.

Pool hopping was one way city kids cooled off on a hot night. When the sun went down, they would put on their swimsuits, jump a fence, quickly slide into an unsuspecting neighbor's pool, jump out just as swiftly, and bolt out of the yard before someone set their dog on them or shot them in the backside with a pellet gun. At least that was the idea.

Towel in hand, I ran downstairs, clothed in my bathing suit and a T-shirt.

"I'm heading out with my friends," I said as I opened the door to leave.

"Hold on a sec," she said calmly. "I want to tell you something."

Methodically, she shut off the faucet and dried her hands with a dishtowel. Then she looked me dead in the eye.

"I want you to know that I trust you, Derek," she said without skipping a beat. "The day you break that bond of trust might be the day you never get it back."

My other foot never hit the top step. I stood there dumbfounded for a second, which seemed like minutes. Then I stepped back into the kitchen, closed the door behind me, and walked over to the window.

"I'm not coming," I yelled down to my buddies. "I have to stay in for the night."

I didn't say a word to Mom, and she said nothing more to me. She knew she had taught me one of the most important lessons of all—that trust is not just hard to earn; it can be lost in a minute.

That's a lesson I remember every single day when I'm dealing with my clients' investments.

Swapping Financial Advisors

Whomever you choose as your financial advisor should share that level of caring and have the competence, credentials, and vision to merit your trust. Should you realize that the financial captain you've been with either doesn't measure up or is no longer working out, it's okay to switch. Remember, financial planning is about your assets and your game plan, so you need to be confident in both the process and the one steering the ship.

Should you decide that another captain makes more sense, I suggest reaching out ahead of any transfer of assets or broker change. After thanking them for their service, just say:

> *Please be advised that we're doing some different planning with an independent planning firm that was highly endorsed by a [friend/family member/trusted advisor]. Please process any transfer accordingly. We thank you in advance for handling the transfer in a timely manner.*
>
> *With appreciation,*
> *Your signature*

This can be done via phone or email.

Top of Mind

In the end, you want a financial planner who will guide you in the financial marketplace and always put your well-being first, whether this involves insurance, planning, portfolio construction, or wealth management. And that's just the start. You also need an advisor and a firm that, like Beauport, has a strategy to help people reach their retirement goals and another one to transition them from the retirement planning phase to the actual retirement itself. And those tactics couldn't be more different.

So, when you're deciding who is going to captain your financial ship, you have to factor in all the things that the captain must do. Your decision needs to be based less on how much the captain is charging compared to someone else and more on what you're going to get for your money. It's not just about the return on the portfolio, it's about everything that that money does. So, you need to have conversations with your planner about risk, opportunities, taxes, values, insurance, inheritance, gifting, philanthropy, and more. That's what the rest of this book is about.

For now, just keep in mind that once you choose a seasoned, respected financial planner who puts you—rather than themselves—first, you owe it to your future financial success to think as much about what you're going to do with your assets as how to accumulate them. It's fine to have a vessel, crew, and gear if you're setting out on a fishing expedition, but somebody has to know how to sell the fish. And before that, they need to have a reliable navigation plan. I'll talk about charting your course with the help of a reliable process and a custom plan in the next chapter.

CATCH OF THE DAY:

- Work with a planner not just to create the plan but to implement it, manage it, and make it an ongoing reality. Plans are great, but they're neither powerful nor practical if they sit on a shelf or in a folder as a concept. Trust, timing, and chemistry are the essential ingredients of a successful and mutually beneficial relationship.
- Find a different captain to steer your ship if trust has been broken, if core competencies do not line up with the services you seek, or if your financial concerns aren't coming first.

CHAPTER 3

CHARTING YOUR COURSE

Have you ever gone on a fishing trip? What did you do to prepare for the day at sea? Check the weather forecast, grab some tackle, some bait, gas up the boat, pack food and water, check and double-check the boat for safety gear, make sure the rods and reels are in good working order, grab the sunglasses and the sunscreen, plan a few different spots in which to fish, etc.

Clearly, quite a bit goes into such an outing, be it a day trip or a more extended stint at sea.

What if you had to catch fish to provide sustenance for your family? Would you have done anything differently to prepare for the trip? What if you had to catch swordfish? Could you do it? Unless you're a professional swordfisherman like my dad, the answer is, of course, that you couldn't. And unless you've got a competent captain and a navigation plan, the same applies to investing well and crafting an income plan for your retirement.

Investing is not a recreational hobby, especially when you're investing for your final financial journey called retirement. You need a purposeful game plan just as much as my dad needed a sturdy vessel, a competent crew, and a safe way to reach his waypoint and get back to the dock with the catch.

Your retirement assets aren't just going to show up and build up on their own. You need a plan and a number (also known as a goal). I find most folks have either an accumulation number ("I want $5 million saved") or an age where they draw the line for earned income work ("I will work till 67 and that's it"). Without that plan, not only do you lack direction, but you also have no way of assessing whether you're on target in terms of not outliving your money.

If you're a typical American retiree, you will need to prepare well before the voyage—a 30-year expedition of both calm seas and tumultuous weather. The average retiree in this country who is married and healthy, in their early 60s, has a greater than 50 percent chance of reaching their 90th birthday. That longevity comes with a price tag, one that many haven't been saving or planning for.

There are roughly 40 million Americans now over the age of 50 who find themselves getting ready to embark on this retirement trip of a lifetime. Yet so many have no idea what to pack for their retirement, what to wear or do, or who to call to captain their ship and help set a safe, reliable course. In short, they have assets but no game plan—or income plan—to ensure success.

Rudderless ships with no captain or too many captains usually wind up with chaos onboard shortly after shoving off or don't wind up setting out to sea at all. But ships are not meant to stay at the dock unattended. In fact, they sink twice as often at dock than they do when they're underway, mostly due to negligence.

Your investment ship is no different. It's designed to be launched with a specific purpose and destination in mind and to navigate the financial seas rather than sitting idle at the dock. In Chapter 1, we talked about figuring out why you're saving money and investing. For my Dad, it was all about not wanting to still have to "bust his ass" and fish at age 67. Your purpose may well be different than Dad's. But, just like him, you have to figure out how to achieve your stated goal.

A first-rate financial captain can help you figure that out since they will be concerned with a whole lot more than just leaving the dock to catch fish and make money. They know that just because you get prepped for a fishing trip and set out, you don't necessarily know where you're headed, when you need to alter the bait or the fishing spot, or how long you want to stay out. Is it until the fuel (i.e., your energy level and/or willingness to keep at it) runs dry or simply once you have filled the boat with fish? Or are there other factors, such as an impending storm?

Additional considerations when coming up with a reliable process include setting a course, the safety of crew and self, how the boat is taking the weather, carrying out the catch plan (25,000 pounds of swordfish was the catch goal for

Dad, for example), determining whether everyone will hold up well if you push the envelope and try to fish one last set before heading home, and getting back to the home port with the boat intact, and the crew healthy and anxious to see what price per pound you get at the fish broker's dock. Five bucks a pound was usually the price in the mid-'80s at the dock.

At the risk of repeating myself, let's review this in terms of you and your financial future. You have to identify why you're fishing and what the goal is. You need an advisor who can help captain your financial ship. And you and the captain must determine what you're fishing for since that will help you figure out when to set out and where to target. In short, you have to know where you're going, because if you don't know your destination, you can end up anywhere.

"If one does not know to which port one is sailing, no wind is favorable," the philosopher Seneca wrote. My dad can vouch for that.

One thing Dad figured out well before becoming a sword captain was the fact that every time the boat left the dock, there needed to be a navigational plan in place, with a bunch of targeted areas in which to fish. Dad needed to know what navigational instruments were essential to help him reach the waypoint (the coordinates of a specific location along the line of travel) and ensure success. This was not a time for generalizations. The waypoint had to be shared with the Coast Guard upon leaving port, so that in the event of a tragedy, they would know where to start looking for the boat.

Captain Charlie also had to make sure that the navigational tools, along with all the gear—including the engine, outriggers, buoy beacon, ice machine, and radio (for communication)—were functional. So, there was quite a bit of preparation done before the boat ever pushed off from the dock.

The start and end of Dad's long commute past the breakwater.

It was a given that the boat didn't leave until both the owner and captain had gone through processes and checklists to ensure a safe voyage. Dad knew that a mistake out at sea could cost him not just that month's income, but his life and the lives of his crew. He had to get it right.

You're in the same boat but for a different reason. If planned correctly, you will retire just once. Unless you change your mind, the first time you choose to do it should be the last, at least financially speaking. So, it's imperative to get it right. That's not easy since it's not like you've been able to practice retiring. Unfortunately, not everyone seeks tried-and-true counsel or puts together a solid financial plan. That oversight can prove costly. Think taxes, fees, opportunity costs where you miss out on a good bet, misallocation where your funds aren't appropriately invested, and market exposure where you're risking too much. As we've seen, not having a captain also increases the likelihood of basing financial decisions on emotions rather than data or expertise.

Consider the couple featured in a 2009 *Wall Street Journal* article just after the Great Recession. While the financial seas remained seriously rough that year, like so many others, they decided to jump ship. Unwilling to risk further loss after taking a $75,000 hit on a Lehman Brothers bond following the collapse of the brokerage firm, the 63-year-old retired real estate broker and 68-year-old pharmacist pulled the last of their stock mutual funds out of the market on May 20, 2009. At the time, nobody knew that March 9, 2009, would prove to be the bottom of the market's decline. In essence, they sold while in the trough of the wave because they could not see land or the horizon or anything promising at the time.

By not having—or adhering to—a financial plan, they not only jumped ship in their survival suits, but they also sank the boat. The result? At worst, the couple missed one of the most historic bull market opportunities of their lifetime. By 2018, the market, which was at 6,600 (DJIA) points when the couple bailed, had climbed to 25,000 points. That's almost a 19,000-point and 300-percent rise in nine years.

By moving all their money to bonds, certificates of deposit, and fixed-rate annuities, they likely made 3 to 4 percent. When you factor in taxes and an inflation rate of 3 percent, it's probably safe to assume that they were treading water at best and slowly sinking financially at worst. Even if they managed to scramble back into the boat at a later date, the asset prices would have been much higher since they had sold near the low.

Major, emotionally driven investment decisions can have significant financial consequences, good and bad.

What would have happened had they donned their life jackets yet remained aboard? Let's assume the couple cashed out $2 million in stocks when the market bottomed out in 2009. If they had left that $2 million in the market, it could have been worth millions more, which puts into perspective that $75,000 Lehman bond loss.

In short, they made a very serious decision that yielded very painful financial consequences. They either weren't operating according to a plan that dictated what the process would be, or they threw the plan out the window. Instead of getting out once they hit a specific number, they waited for their stocks and bonds to go down hundreds of thousands of dollars on paper during one of, if not *the,* most chaotic time of their financial lives before bailing. That tells me they got scared and transferred that fear to their investments.

It bears repeating that they certainly were not alone. People all over the country cashed out their retirement accounts at the bottom of the trough, turning paper losses into real ones. Sure, you have time to make up those losses if you're still in your 40s and 50s. But at a certain point in your life, there is little to no coming back from this. If you're in your 60s and 70s, you simply can't afford to let your money earn 4 percent when you know you need an 8 percent return to live a full life.

Of course, all these decisions imply that you have a number in your head that you're either aiming for or have reached.

As mentioned earlier, almost everyone has a number or an age at which they're going to retire. Some people focus on how much money they want a month after they stop working. Others know how large their nest egg needs to be before they can retire.

If your number, whatever it is, works, then great. You're on your way to coming up with a sound financial plan. All too often, however, the number hasn't been well thought out.

"If I acquire three more rental properties, I can retire and live on the income they generate," one woman told me. Of course, that means she's putting all her eggs in a single basket, in this case, real estate, because that's what she knows and is comfortable with. But has she factored in the carrying costs, including interest payments, taxes, insurance, and repairs? What if the property sits vacant for a while, and she's not getting that monthly check to cover the mortgage? What happens if the rental market dries up or becomes super competitive due to tons of inventory and she has to cut the rents? Or what if she simply tires of being a landlord? Oops.

"Let's take 10 percent out of my account each year as a distribution," another person told me. "I should be all set because that is what the markets have done, and I will still have my principle remaining after Year 10." Big mistake, since he's forgotten to account for taxes and inflation, along with stagnate or negative market returns.

Coming up with a number that works for you involves figuring out your priorities as well as decisions about how you're going to reach your goal. And yes, that usually means that you're going to need to sacrifice here and there.

When my wife Karen and I came up with our number, we realized we would need to buckle down to get there. With three kids to educate, we knew we were in for some whopper expenses before we retired, even though we believe in them having some skin in the game and sharing in some of the cost for college. We set up 529 savings plans for their education as soon as the kids had Social Security numbers and committed to a monthly amount to keep that process consistent and mindless. Regardless of what the market was doing, we bought shares every 30 days with the amount we had agreed on, a risk-reduction investment practice known as dollar-cost averaging since the months when shares cost a lot are balanced out by other months when you get a great deal. And voila! By the time our oldest boy turned 17, he had two years fully funded before he ever set foot on campus.

The college funds are just the start. As 40-somethings, we decided not to rely on Social Security or pensions for our retirement. Considering the way both are going, that just seemed too risky. After factoring this into our number, we realized that we needed to save north of 15 percent of our income, which meant we were going to have to make some sacrifices. As a result, my wife drove our 2006 Caravan for 14 years. When Karen handed it over for the kids to beat on as they learned to drive, it had 180,000 miles on it. It now has topped 200,000 miles.

That's far from our only compromise. We didn't dine out much. We didn't take the kids to Disney World, even though I'm sure we would've all loved it. Instead, we earmarked a certain amount of savings to take a yearly family trip, so we could all take a break from busy calendars and be in a new place for seven days discovering things together. Otherwise, we just hung at the lake where my in-laws bought a modest vacation home.

When they initially purchased the lakeside house, hoping the extended family would gather there, I was a member of a local golf club. I love the sport and it was a great way to meet with clients. But I realized it was cutting into our family time, and that I would wind up spending thousands of dollars on golf over the next 10 years. So, I gave up the golf membership and purchased a small bass fishing boat instead, a trade-off I don't regret for a minute since I regularly go out with whichever family member happens to be on the dock.

Living for today and planning for tomorrow is a delicate balance. One of my guilty pleasures is wine—Napa Cabs and Spanish reds in particular—so I had a wine cave installed at home. Sliding open the railed oak door, walking into this little area in the basement, and seeing an abundance of stacked bottles to both enjoy and share brings me and my wife (and others, too) great pleasure. Sure, that money could have gone elsewhere, but you've got to live a little. Since I could afford—and budget for—this bit of luxury, while continuing to save our targeted monthly amount, I indulged myself. Had that not been the case, I wouldn't have, or I would have waited until I could splurge without compromising other financial goals.

Finding Your Sweet Spot
Just as everyone has a number, everyone has a sweet spot, where the right plan comes together. Take me. From the time I was in junior high, I knew I wanted to be a businessman. Somehow, I detoured into teaching, which planted a different kind of seed. Three years later, I returned to the financial planning career I was always meant for. But the teaching-related insights I brought with me would forever influence how I did that job. It wasn't enough to just invest people's money for them. I wanted to educate them about the process, just as I want to encourage financial literacy in our kids.

As someone who lives in the world of finance, I see the benefits of planning and the shortfalls of faulty or nonexistent planning all the time. However, I learned about the need to save money for the future long before I ever got in the business. On my 7th birthday, my Nana took me to the local savings bank to open up my first passbook savings account with a $10 deposit, a practice my wife and I have carried on with our children.

"It's important to save little chunks today for a bigger goal later," Nana told me.

A faithful, dedicated single mother of seven children, she had very little in the way of financial resources. Still, she managed to live on less than 100 percent of what she had and imparted great wisdom to her grandson at an impressionable age. Lesson learned. Life's a journey, I realized, and saving for it was necessary.

The same holds for retirement. Fortunately, little bits of financial pain and sacrifice pay off, adding up to lots more dollars later on. And that has everything to do with how well you can live during those golden years.

I remember sitting down with clients in their 60s who were worth many millions. They shared with me part of the secret to their success.

"We sat at this very table when we were in our 30s and decided that we didn't want to work hard in our 70s," the wife told me. "So, we decided to stay put and renovate this house instead of buying a bigger one with a bigger mortgage. That allowed us to max out our 401K plans. It turned out to be a good move."

That purpose and clarity of vision allowed them to stick to a game plan that dictated their saving, spending, and investing habits. As a result, they have plenty on which to live well now that they're no longer working, and to leave a legacy once they're gone.

I have had the opportunity to work with many such financially successful, goal-oriented people. And I've learned that few get there overnight. Most reap their just rewards years down the road after some pain and struggle, along with the resilience to weather financial storms. And it all starts with a number and a plan.

What's your number? You know you've got one—an asset level to reach, a date to retire, or how much income you desire annually so you can maintain a particular lifestyle. That number is sort of like your ideal weight goal. We have a number. Similarly, most of us have some kind of financial number or range in our heads. We tell ourselves, "Once I hit $3 million, I can call it quits and live off the interest or just work part-time." Or, "At 66, I can earn what I want and not have my Social Security benefits affected, so that's when I will slow it down."

In his 1990 book, *P.S. I Love You,* H. Jackson Brown remembers advice his mother gave him, which over the years has been incorrectly attributed to Mark Twain:

> *Twenty years from now you will be more disappointed by the things that you didn't do than by the ones you did do. So throw off the bowlines!*
>
> *Sail away from the safe harbor. Catch the trade winds in your sails.*
>
> *Explore. Dream. Discover!*

Sounds wonderfully inspiring, doesn't it? Literally speaking, you might picture yourself wearing the proper yachting attire on a beautiful blue-bird day, setting sail with an ocean breeze blowing through your hair, staring at the horizon wondering what's out there in the distance, and hearing nothing but the sound of saltwater splashing against the hull of your vessel. Figuratively speaking, you may picture yourself accomplishing one of those personal bucket-list items you have mentally jotted down in your head or just simply trying out a new experience that draws you out of your comfort zone.

From a practical standpoint, I would first ask these questions:

- Where do you want to go?
- How will you arrive at your destination?
- What will you do once safely there?
- Who will you be with, and how long will you stay?
- Why are we going anyway? What's the purpose of the voyage?
- Who do you want to take care of? Yourself? Your family?
- And finally, what's it going to cost?

In short, the number you need to aim for depends on you defining what your vision is going to look like. If you're going to realize that dream, you can't afford to wait before putting together the right plan because the only thing riskier than navigating the financial seas is not setting sail at all.

No matter what your number(s), you had better be prepared to cast your lines in the right fishing spot because getting close isn't good enough in finance or in fishing.

One day, back when Dad was still fishing as a crew member rather than a captain, another vessel lay just half a mile to the port side. The neighboring boat hauled in more than 50 huge swordfish. Dad's boat caught less than 10 of any notable size—and not all of those were even swordfish. It turned out that the other boat had cast its lines in 68-degree water, while the lines on Dad's boat had been cast a little deeper, which meant the hooks were in 65-degree water. They were both right on top of the fish, but casting their bait at the wrong depth in a temperature that was just three degrees too chilly cost each of the crew members on Dad's boat thousands of dollars. In an ocean of 139.7 million square miles, being only eight football fields away from the other boat was not close enough, a lesson Dad would never forget when he charted course after course as captain of the Andrea Gail.

Dad was always trying to get to a number during those years. If he met his target of 25,000 pounds of fish and the average price for fish was $4 to $5 per pound, the boat could often gross $125,000 in fish sales. Deduct some $25,000 in trip expenses off the top for fuel, gear, food, equipment, etc., and you were left with $100,000, half of which went to the boat owner. That left $50,000 to split among five guys. Since the captain gets two shares, that meant that each of the other four men would receive more than $8,000, with the captain getting double that, for one month of fishing. Not bad!

The swordfish was certainly the prize, but it was never about the fish, really, just as saving for retirement isn't about how much you accumulate but rather the lifestyle you can lead and the legacy you can leave. For my dad, the importance lay in what the swordfish represented: shelter for his family, a car for reliable transportation, food, clothes, funds to cover insurance premiums, a family night out, and maybe even a vacation for mom and us kids. The swordfish itself was the means to an end, and every pound harvested provided a bit of economic freedom and opportunity for him and his crew. Considering that he only had from April to October to reap the harvest and provide for a family of five, he needed to have as close to a foolproof plan as possible.

Of course, he and his crew knew what species of fish they were targeting and where they should be, which was a solid start. They also understood that the swordfish is biologically wired to leave its East Coast winter mating area of the Gulf of Mexico as the water temperatures rise. It follows the warm current of the Gulf Stream to its northern edges in search of food and returns in the late summer or early fall to the Gulf of Mexico to repeat the process all over again.

To capitalize on this knowledge, Dad's plan also had to account for gear, supplies, and bait specific to the targeted catch, along with enough fuel and provisions for the trip and a little extra too, just in case. He also had to factor in conditions. He knew he could rely on lighthouse beacons to help ensure safety, which was reassuring since even the greatest ship crew and captain need help in tough times. Not wanting that kind of emergency to be routine, he planned accordingly, determined that his livelihood on the unpredictable seas be as predictable as possible.

Finally, unlike investing in the financial markets, he couldn't fish just anywhere. He had to factor in fishing regulations, which determined where in the North Atlantic Canadian versus U.S. fishing fleets were allowed to fish. Knowing that a four-day or so steam at about 10 knots would get him to the southern tail of the Grand Banks—right where the Gulf Stream meets the Bank some 1,100 to 1,200 nautical miles from Gloucester Harbor—he would set off due east as soon as he cleared the Gloucester harbor break wall. While that seems crazy since their destination lay to the north, he knew that north of the equator, the earth's curvature tends to push you north as you navigate east. So that was the rhumbline (technically not the shortest distance from point A to point B, but the shortest distance between Gloucester Harbor and the Grand Banks once the earth's curvature had been taken into account).

Dad would set the coordinates—42 degrees west longitude and 43 degrees north latitude—into the APS automatic pilot system connected to the gyrocompass. This was never a set-it-and-forget-it deal. The boat's position had to be checked and modified every half hour at the most, as one degree off early on in the voyage turns into many hundreds of miles away from your destination later on.

That wasn't the only thing he and the crew had to watch out for. Although the ocean is vast, debris, other fishing vessels, cargo ships, along with waves, storms, and wind all presented potential threats. Dad and each crew member took two-hour watches to make sure they stayed on course and safe, using everything from the LORAN (short for long-range navigation) system's radio signals, along with weather fax and national weather service intel, to help plot the course and keep updated.

When they finally reached their destination, the crew was always itching to put the lines in and fish. But first, Dad had to put the boat in position—no fish finder out there, just a good sense of the predictable patterns of the hungry swordfish and where they like to be and/or feed. Setting out the line and then hauling it back in was a two-day commitment, so starting in the right place was critical. That meant locating water that was 67 to 69 degrees. Anything colder and he'd land nothing but sharks. First, they'd ascertain the water temperature and depth with a thermometer on a long string marked with tape to denote each fathom (six feet). Eventually, a paravane—a 300-pound lead-filled, bird-like structure attached to a steel cable—reported thermal temperature and depth.

Once they reached their destination, it was time to thread the frozen mackerel and squid onto the hooks with the utmost care, so when the thrashing swordfish knocked its prey to stun it, the bait wouldn't fall off the hook and provide an easy snack for the hungry swordfish. That, too, is part of the art of swordfishing.

Some less-than-stellar captains, known as *slipper skippers*, ruled from their pilothouse castle. Once they stepped foot in the wheelhouse, their rugged fishing boots came off, and their warm cozy house slippers went on, never to see the dirty work deck of their own ship. That wasn't Dad. He knew that the mental part of fishing is as important as the physical. Just think about it. He was in the elements on a 72-foot stainless steel vessel in sparse quarters with two beds—one for the captain and one for the engineer. His only amenity was that there were only two of them bunking in his room rather than four. But Dad wasn't in his bed much anyway—he knew he would get little sleep despite having to withstand hard labor. If morale tanked, and why wouldn't it if the captain didn't care enough to involve himself in the dirty work, that virus spread fast and even a good trip would be spoiled.

That sure wasn't for Dad. He worked right alongside his crew during every phase of the operation. But the boat had a finite amount of fuel and could only hold 40,000 pounds of fish. Once he hit that limit or the tank dropped to a certain level, he had to head back to the dock. This is where the fishing-finance analogy no longer holds. As a fisherman, you can always work another year and make more money or, if you have a game plan, you can go on to the next adventure. Ultimately, however, there's only so much you can do. With money, there's no limit on good. There's only a limit on time, so you want to come up with a financial game plan that will allow you to carve out all the moments you need for what's important.

Charting your Financial Course

Having a front-row seat during the last three recessions and over the last two-plus decades as a practitioner in the income-planning business, I've learned that a financially successful retirement has as much to do with having saved "enough" as it does with having a tangible game plan that will deliver for 30 years. How to do that is easy enough. The internet or a conversation with a financially savvy friend can help you figure out the basics regarding what to invest in. The list of options isn't as long as one might think, so let's cut right to the chase here and spell those out. When it comes to investments, there are:

- **Stocks**
  A stock represents a piece of ownership in a company, allowing for voting privileges and dividends if applicable. Understandably, since there are small, mid-sized, and large capitalized companies, the stocks of those companies are categorized respectively as small-cap, mid-cap, and large-cap (also known as big-cap). Think of it like this. With a capitalization of more than $53 billion, Ford Motor is defined as a large company, so its stock is classified as large-cap. The company that makes the airbags Ford puts in their vehicles has a market capitalization of just over $9.5 billion, so its stock is classified as small-cap. Should its market valuation rise over the $10 billion mark, it would be classified as a mid-cap. We'll talk more about why this matters later in the book. For now, just keep in mind that as an investor, you ride the up-and-down wave of how well or poorly the stock price performs.

- **Bonds**
  A bond is debt issued by a company or government agency. You don't own a piece of the company or agency; you're loaning capital to them in return for bond interest and expected return of capital investment with or without appreciation or depreciation.

- **Mutual funds/Index funds**
  A mutual fund is a diversified, managed portfolio of stocks and/or bonds (or both) offered by financial companies that employ money managers to build and manage a portfolio with a defined purpose (growth, income, internationally focused, mid-sized companies, etc.) An index fund is an unmanaged fund that tracks

a specific segment—or index—of the market, such as healthcare, international, or the S&P 500. Because they're unmanaged, they have low associated fees. Conversely, many mutual funds have sales charges and ongoing operating costs higher than respective Exchange Traded Funds (ETFs—see below), and only about 10 percent of actively managed funds outperform the respective index they track over a 20-year period, according to 2022 New York Times piece. So, if you're going to opt for mutual funds, you need to find the great ones. In addition, mutual funds are usually less tax-efficient than ETFs, and as a general rule more expensive than ETFs both to own and to purchase.

- **Exchange Traded Funds**
  Known as ETFs, these are potentially beneficial for taxable accounts, providing a low-cost alternative to mutual funds and a more diversified option than just a single stock or bond. An ETF is a basket of stocks or bonds that usually tracks some market index (S&P 500, Russell, international, small-caps, etc.) or industry sector (healthcare, dividend payors, tech, industrials, etc.). An ETF can be managed (active, with companies being weighted differently) or passive (static, created to follow a specific model. ETFs are created by financial institutions and have significantly increased their market share in the last decade relative to traditional mutual funds. Sometimes dozens of positions are included in an ETF; other times, hundreds of companies comprise the ETF. Since these are not owned inside a mutual fund structure, ETFs boast a unique cost basis at the time of purchase and are priced throughout the trading day like

a stock or bond rather than at the close of the market like mutual funds.

- **Commodities**
  A raw material or primary agricultural product that can be bought and sold, such as copper or coffee.

- **Real estate**
  Maintenance costs need to be factored into this investment.

- **Currency**
  Due to the volatility of currency, this works only for investors who are ready to pivot super quickly. On the other hand, ETFs and mutual funds can be a way to invest in currency with registered products.

- **Collectibles**
  Collectibles range from art, jewelry, and automobiles to stamps, comic books, baseball cards, and even vintage toasters. You'll need to maintain your investment (keeping it clean and free of wear and tear) to retain value. The market—and therefore the value—of these collectibles, however, waxes and wanes. On the other hand, the entry level can be modest, as long as you avoid counterfeits.

Of course, there's an art to figuring out how to balance all these kinds of investments, which we'll talk about in this and upcoming chapters. But to come up with a plan that will prompt you to stay the course or chart a new one, you need to decide what you want to own and come up with a financial plan based on your *why*. That's the only way you'll create something that has value and meaning to you.

So why do you want to invest, save, protect, and insure anyway?

Some reasonable answers for investing could simply be to combat inflation, save on taxes, finance a large purchase, come up with a down payment on a home, buy a vacation home on the waterfront, educate your children, or invest in the future of the planet (perhaps your legacy?) with socially responsible companies. Regardless of why you're investing, you'll quickly figure out that the "safe" place to put your money will usually yield low returns because of low risk, which we'll talk about in Chapter 4. For now, just remember that the right investment has to balance risk with the returns you seek—and all of that could change as the years pass and your goals shift.

Either way, you need a plan. The plan will never be perfect at the outset due to the imperfect storm called retirement. We all aim for Plan A and end up with Plans B, C, or D. Even so, we have to get started, analysis paralysis notwithstanding. Don't wait for your financial ship to come in. For the inheritance to land. For your business to be sold. For those lottery numbers to finally hit. For your child to get older and be close to college age. It's time to push off the dock and go. Now!

Yes, it's time to come up with a plan that's as good as you can make it for now. A plan, however, only works if it's practical, strategic, and if you can stick with it. That's where certified financial planners come in. We help people achieve clarity about their why—their purpose—and then develop a plan that honors that.

With a new client, I always start by asking about their feelings related to money. I ask about their favorite or most important memory as it relates to money. I ask about their most painful memory as it relates to money. Maybe that involved their father losing his job and the family being hungry for six months before he found work again. The answers, whatever they might be, help me understand people's psychology when it comes to money and investing.

Then I ask them about their goals and expectations. We don't just look at their financial situation and their attitude about risk; we talk about their values and their priorities. I do the same thing during annual check-ins with all my clients, no matter how long they've been with me, but only after we've talked about what's going on with their lives. It gets personal in a hurry. Money always does.

Regardless of what is happening in the short run, all parties need to have some element of a long-term perspective for clarity when developing a plan. That starts with realizing that retirement is a multi-decade-long endeavor and that you'll need more than just a target number to live in dignity and independence for 30 years. Too many investors and pre-retirees are only focused, if focused at all, on the asset accumulation figure they feel they need to reach before they can call themselves retired. Getting there, however, requires discipline, monitoring, correct placement of assets for accumulation and distribution, and ultimately some meaningful assignment and purpose related to creating something important such as lifestyle, legacy, or gifting, to name a few.

Once I understand where my clients are coming from—their *why*—I analyze their financial situation, including assets, liabilities and cash flow, projected retirement income, current insurance coverage, investments, tax strategies, and estate planning. To determine how best to meet their goals, we ask them to fill out one of two questionnaires. If you're in your 50s or younger, the ARC™ Questionnaire on the next two pages will help you figure out where you're at and what you need to do. You want to retire at 62 and withdraw $100,000 a year? Then you'd better figure out how much you need to save each year. It will also help to make sure that you're protecting the machine that's funding the retirement (i.e., you) with life and disability insurance.

ARC™ QUESTIONNAIRE

Client Information

	Name	Gender	Date of Birth	State of Residence	Risk Class
Client 1					
Client 2					

Pre-Retirement Information

Type	Annual Gross Income	Occupation / Income Title	Expected Annual Increase	Retirement / End Age
Earned Income (Client 1)	$		%	
Earned Income (Client 2)	$		%	
Other *(e.g. rental property, royalties, part-time work)*	$		%	
Other *(e.g. rental property, royalties, part-time work)*	$		%	

Expenses

Annual Expenses (not including debts below)	Inflation Adjustment
$	%

Debt

Debt Name (mortgage, credit card, etc.)	Remaining Balance Due	Current Annual Payment	Remaining Years of Payments	Interest Rate
	$	$		%
	$	$		%
	$	$		%
	$	$		%

Retirement Assumptions

Income Goals	
Please provide either Gross, After-Tax, or Replacement Ratio	
Annual Gross Income *(today's dollars)*	$
Annual After-Tax *(today's dollars)*	$
Replacement Ratio of Current Gross Income	%

Expectations	
Years of Retirement	
Pre-Retirement Growth Rate	%
Post Retirement Growth Rate	%
Annual Inflation Adjustment	%

Alternative Scenario

If retirement is not achievable under the assumptions listed above, please select one of the following adjustments:

☐ Spend Less   ☐ Retire Later   ☐ Combination

Post-Retirement Income Sources

Type	Owner	Yearly Income	Inflation Adjustment	Age Income Begins	Age Ends *(if applicable)*
Social Security		$	%		
Social Security		$	%		
Other *(specify in notes section)*		$	%		
Other *(specify in notes section)*		$	%		

(1 of 2)

ARC™ QUESTIONNAIRE CONT.

Assets

Asset Name (i.e 401(k), Roth IRA, Brokerage)	Owner	Asset Value	Annual Contributions	Contributed By (Client, Spouse, Employer)
		$	$	
		$	$	
		$	$	
		$	$	
		$	$	
		$	$	
		$	$	

Cash Reserves (i.e Checkings, Savings, other)	Owner	Amount	Annual Contribution
		$	$
		$	$
		$	$

Education Funding

Names of Children	Date of Birth	Annual Tuition (today's dollars)	Years in College	Tuition Inflation	Current Savings for Child	Current Contributions
		$		%	$	$
		$		%	$	$
		$		%	$	$
		$		%	$	$

Insurance Policies

Type (i.e Life, Long Term Care)	Insured	Annual Premium	Premium Duration	Benefits	Cash Value	Inflation Adjustment (LTC only)*
		$			$	%
		$			$	%
		$			$	%
		$			$	%

*Inflation Adjustment for LTC is assumed to be compound growth unless stated in the notes

Additional Notes

All too often, we think about retiring *from* something rather than retiring *into* something. The objective is to trade up to an even more meaningful life, one with a purpose that aligns with your values as well as your deepest desires. To help make that happen, once you're a few years away from retiring or getting ready to enter retirement, it's time to take everything you've saved, everything you've invested, everything you've allocated, and speak to a competent captain to manage this last financial journey. The financial captain's role is to make sure the risks have been navigated so you have the best chance to live this final voyage in the best possible way as you meet your living needs, your giving needs, and your purpose.

But how do you set yourself up for that? How do you turn all your "stuff" into $7,500 a month of income (or whatever your number is) to replace the earned income you had while working? What does this look like for the next 25 years? The RISK™ Questionnaire on the next two pages can help, starting with simply figuring out precisely what you've squirreled away.

RISK™ QUESTIONNAIRE

Client Information

	First Name	Last Name	Gender	Date of Birth	State	Retirement Age
Client 1:						
Client 2:						

Retirement Goals

Permanent Expenses	Annual Amount	
A. What annual amount will fund your needs (e.g. utilities, food, etc)	$	(after-tax)
B. What annual amount will fund your wants (e.g. entertainment, travel, etc)	$	(after-tax)
Total annual spending in retirement (sum of A+B above)	$	(after-tax)

Fluctuating Expenses

Please include notes on any fluctuating expenses you would like reflected (e.g., $30k wedding in 2 years, $25k car every 5 years, etc.)

Income Sources

Type (Social Security, Pension, Rent, etc)	Owner	Gross Annual Income	Age Income Begins	Age Income Ends	Inflation Adjustment %	Pension Survivorship Feature	If Govt Pension, # of Substantial Earning Years (or attach Social Security statement)
		$			%		
		$			%		
		$			%		
		$			%		

Assets

Account Name	Registration (IRA, Roth, NQ, etc)	Owner	Account Value	Allocation (Conservative, Moderate, or Aggressive)	Annual Contribution until Retirement	If it's a future lump sum, include the year it's received
			$		$	
			$		$	
			$		$	
			$		$	
			$		$	
			$		$	
			$		$	

RISK™ QUESTIONNAIRE

Insurance Policies (if applicable)

	Policy 1	Policy 2	Policy 3	Policy 4
Insurance Type (Life, Life with LTC Rider, or Long Term Care)				
Solution Name				
Insured				
Annual Premium	$	$	$	$
Premium Duration				
Death Benefit	$	$	$	$
Cash Value	$	$	$	$
Inflation Adjustment	%	%	%	%
Inflation Type (Compound or Simple)				
LTC Rider Percentage	%	%	%	%

Risk Rankings

Please Rank the Risks below from 1–6 with the Highest Priority being 1 (Please use each number only once)	Rank
Market Sequence of Returns: The risk of retiring in the wrong year (e.g. retiring just before the Great Depression)	
Longevity: The risk I will outlive the assets I have set aside for retirement	
Health: The risk I will be forced to deplete a significant portion of my assets to pay for long term care	
Inflation: The risk that the cost of goods and services will increase over time	
Liquidity: The risk my current portfolio provides me limited or no flexibility when unexpected needs arise	
Survivor: The risk of leaving a financial burden on loved ones	

Notes

Helping my clients gain clarity about what they have and what they're aiming for allows us to work together to determine what we need to do. It also helps them stick to the plan we come up with. The plan will obviously be determined by where they're at in life, which is exactly what you need to factor in when coming up with your own plan.

The takeaway here is that the older you are and the less time you have to invest, the more saver-oriented and conservative you should be with your assets. The younger you are, and the longer your investment time horizon, the more volatility you can handle. Either way, in the end, a globally diversified wealth plan that includes income and capital appreciation is often a great long-term strategy.

Of course, there are many ways to invest and generate income, which means you can manage your investment portfolio in so many different ways—sole focus on income and dividends, capital appreciation stocks only during your working and accumulation years, alternative investments to generate alpha (higher returns that carry risk comparable to whatever benchmark we're using to measure performance) in your portfolio, small-cap/mid-cap/large-cap, international and emerging markets, balanced portfolios. Just as the ocean is a vast area of saltwater and treasure lying below, the investment arena is just as big and daunting, so you need to know what you seek, create a plan, and follow a process that will lead you to your targeted goal. It serves no purpose to you or your investment game plan to be seeking yields or returns of, say, 7 percent historically and yet allocating your resources to investments that may at best get you 5 percent. You can't go swordfishing with light tackle and small worms as bait—the fish will either pass you by or ruin your gear. Nobody wins in that scenario, and everyone gets frustrated. Again, this speaks to clear expectations, communication, and transparency of your game plan.

"Hey, the stock market is up 20 percent," I hear you saying. "How's my portfolio doing?" That depends, quite frankly, on what you're fishing for. If you are fishing for the DJIA return or the S&P 500 index or Nasdaq, then sure, you will take 100 percent of the risk of that index and get most of the return, net of fees. Most diversified investors take less risk and own various percentages in numerous sectors of the broader market. Should one industry or sector go south, it minimizes the damage done to the entire portfolio. The flip side is true, too. If the tech-heavy Nasdaq index is up 20 percent and your portfolio is up less, this simply means you don't own one sector and aren't taking all the risk that one sector or industry bears.

The all-or-nothing approach can pay off when things are good, but that's a dangerous way to invest and to live. I know. Dad's business was precarious and very particular—fishing for swordfish and swordfish alone, with specific gear, tackle, and bait for that one species. That meant feast or famine. They wouldn't be catching striped bass, nor shrimp, nor codfish considering where and how they were fishing. Most folks don't want to take that risk or be so concentrated with their investment portfolios—feast or famine is not a prudent approach to undertake when you're planning to invest for a child's education, invest for a sufficient retirement nest egg, or create adequate portfolio income for your retirement years.

We'll talk about a number of approaches to investing in this book. But the best plan—and the only one that works—is the one you stick to.

That's not always easy, and I'm not just talking about the inevitable belt-tightening that's required. You have to stay the course, no matter what the distractions or perceived opportunities. There are 2,800 stocks traded on the New York Stock Exchange alone, which means there are thousands of stocks you can buy every single day. Of course, you can't own them all. Your plan has been created based on what you need to fish for. The vessel has been outfitted accordingly.

No matter how much you love lobster, if you need to bring in $150,000, you cannot afford to jump on a lobster boat that holds, at most, 850 pounds since, even if lobsters are selling for an all-time high of $5 at the dock, you won't even make $5,000. Similarly, if your heart is set on catching thousands of pounds of swordfish at $5 a pound, you also can't afford to take that lobster boat to the Grand Banks or rely on a rod and reel to catch all those swordfish. In short and at the risk of repeating myself, just as you can't successfully catch swordfish with a rod and reel or the wrong type of vessel, you won't find success if you invest in financial instruments that pay 2 to 3 percent if your plan dictates you need a 6 to 7 percent rate of return.

Once we've defined your target destination and charted your course, we'll want to consider both investment opportunities and risks before matching your plan with an investment strategy and portfolio. We'll talk about how to make the most of your investing opportunity while minimizing your risk next. That's next.

CATCH OF THE DAY:

- Before the boat leaves the dock, there has to be a specific strategy. It all starts with a plan—your plan. The plan has to be yours, created with your best interests in mind.
- When coming up with your accumulation- or distribution-phase financial plan, begin with your accumulation or income distribution strategy and know exactly what you're fishing for. Most planning is imperfect in some way—adaptation is necessary, especially when things are in motion. Life throws us curveballs and the markets move daily. Make sure your plan takes that into account.
- Having a tactical approach is imperative. Think of it as the difference between running just for exercise versus training for a marathon. There has to be some sort of goal-based plan based on your number, which may fluctuate.
- Don't just look at expenses. You also have to look at risk and return when it comes to investments. Take Dad as an example. Had he just considered the expenses piece, he would have found the cheapest boat and equipment and only remained close to shore. While he would have saved

on expenses with that approach, he wouldn't have caught any of the prized swordfish.
- Have faith in a custom, solid plan, and stay your course. Implement your plan according to the stage of life you're experiencing—accumulating (ARC™) or distributing (RISK™).
- Finally, remember that while navigating the financial seas can be risky, there is treasure at sea, and it will very likely be much less rewarding to never leave the dock.

CHAPTER 4

OCEANS OF OPPORTUNITY AND RISK

THE CHOICES WE MAKE—and don't make—define us and set the path for our future. Nowhere is that truer than where our finances are concerned. Coming up with a plan is a critical first step. But it's not good enough to simply have a bunch of money sitting in a bunch of funds. That is not how you mitigate investment risk. Successful retirement and income planning for you and your heirs is not a do-it-yourself project. Someone has to know how to engineer, align, and rebalance your portfolio with purpose. Just like a boat designed and outfitted to harvest swordfish, you have to leave the dock with a plan, put it into motion, and assess potential dangers along the way to achieve your goals.

Of course, even that doesn't guarantee safety. Think about the couple from the last chapter. Having invested heavily in bonds, which most people think of as safe, they felt they were all set. Then Lehman Brothers, the company backing the bond, went bust, prompting the couple to go to cash and call it quits.

Fixing your income in a rising-cost world can lead to a reduction in purchasing power. Bonds, for example, are not a great investment when interest rates increase. However, when interest rates eventually do fall, bond prices will rise. In short, you need to adapt your strategy to your income needs and the current state of the economy.

What's a retiree to do?

What are *you* going to do?

Do you have a plan for your assets outliving you, and do you rest easy knowing that the ship you're steering will reach its port of call?

Nobody ever comes into our office with a couple million bucks and says, "Hey, take as much risk as you want with this and turn it into four million." No! They've realized, "Okay, I've reached the level I wanted to get to. Now it's time to turn the harvest into treasure that will support me and my goals for whatever time I have left here. I don't need to take additional risks because we've just identified that I've got enough and might even have a surplus."

In investing, as in life, things can go wrong, often when you least expect it. There are the risks you know about and have considered as well as those that happen in the moment. That's why, even when you think your plan is rock solid, you always want to make contingency plans, which you'll learn more about in Chapter 7. My dad figured that out early, well before he had become a swordfishing captain.

By the age of 21, Dad was well versed in risk, having already taken many in his young life—leaving school, moving from home to a grandma's house in another state, getting married, having three children, and then at age 26 becoming a commercial fisherman to support his family.

It's said that commercial fishing is one of the riskiest vocations on the planet. Not only are sword fishermen dealing with Mother Nature's capricious conditions, but their workspace is full of inherent danger: hydraulic machinery, diesel fuel and engines that need maintenance, fishing line, hooks, knives, swordfish swords being handled in rolling North Atlantic waves, and living on a 72-foot steel vessel with no significant landmass around you for hundreds of nautical miles. It's not for the faint of heart.

While it would seem that Dad chose to go after swordfish, it was actually the other way around. As a little boy growing up 30 miles northwest of New York City, he never dreamt of becoming a sword captain and spending a month at a time at sea chasing and harvesting multiple 100-plus-pound fish armed with swords. But when he misbehaved as a teen, having moved in with his maternal grandparents who lived in Gloucester, his punishment was day-fishing with his grandfather. It turns out that Charlie enjoyed working on the water more than going to middle school and sitting at a desk.

By the early '80s, friends already making substantial money in Gloucester's swordfishing industry encouraged him to join. Even though the pay was good, the swordfishing boats were continually looking for quality, able-bodied crew members willing to work the ocean and regularly spend a month away from shore without seasickness or a longing for land. The job was risky, sure. But far riskier, in Dad's mind, was the prospect of staying in a dead-end job for the rest of his life, punching a time clock in a cold storage facility, and moving dead fish around for a meager wage.

Why do that when he could put his physical skills and excellent work ethic to use on the ocean with the potential for a much higher payday? He fell for the lure of swordfishing hook, line, and sinker. He loved the thrill of the hunt and the challenge the vast North Atlantic presented. Even in calm seas, absent any issues on board, the fishing expedition for migratory swordfish among thousands of square miles of ocean always got the blood flowing.

Dog Bar Breakwater – Eastern Point.

He would discover in a very personal way just how risky commercial fishing could be while crewing on the Lancer, a sturdy boat owned by the Hilliards, a longtime fishing family out of Rockport, located adjacent to Gloucester. The 50-footer wasn't a traditional swordfishing boat you would take to the Grand Banks, but the promise of swordfish riches in the Gulf Stream less than a day's steam east proved irresistible. The $80,000 it would take to fix, update, and upgrade the small vessel was deemed worth the investment.

Finally, it was time to take her out. The weather and seas couldn't have been better. So, at 3 a.m. on July 2nd in the mid-1980s, instead of celebrating his wedding anniversary with my mom, Dad set out on the boat which headed to a spot 100 miles off the coast of Cape Cod. When they reached the bountiful fishing area called the Canyons, the ocean was, in my dad's words, "flat-ass calm." With 125 fathoms of Atlantic ocean below, my dad, the boat owner, and two crew members, including a greenhorn teenager on his first fishing trip, went to work.

After eight days at sea, they had already landed 8,000 pounds of fish worth $40,000. Not a bad payday and they weren't done yet. That night, with the seasoned crew member taking the first watch, they set their hooks and crawled into their bunks.

Baboom!

Awakened with a start by the loud thump of something crashing into the boat near the bow, Dad jumped up and ran to the engine room in his long-john PJs to assess any damage and check on the boat's power source. As he looked down into the engine room, he saw water gushing in from the hull, precisely in the restored area they had just spent time fixing with a loan from the boat owner's dad.

The Lancer was holding, but that wouldn't last long. Too much water was coming in too quickly for the bilge pumps to keep up, and the engine room was filling up noticeably. With no way to fix the damage, they had only one alternative. Abandon ship.

Fortunately, and even though it was their first time out together, the crew had a process. Sometimes what makes a great fisherman is not just charting the correct course and hitting the fish; it's knowing how to survive the storm and what to do in dire circumstances, so you save your butt and get home safely. Before the boat had left the dock, all crew members had been briefed on exactly where the survival suits were and how to put them on. They didn't need to ask where the strobe lights or the life rafts were. The fact that the boat was sinking didn't prompt screams or panic. Instead, with no time to think, they simply did what they needed to do.

Having ascertained that the boat was no longer viable, the captain issued a mayday-mayday call over the radio, shot a flare gun twice into the night sky, and directed all members to put on their survival suits. By then, the boat was going down quickly. Having grabbed the strobe light along with the flare gun and cartridge, they deployed the lifeboat.

Now, the greenhorn didn't exactly exhibit the quiet, calm professionalism of my dad and the rest of the crew. Noticeably scared, he had to be talked into jumping into the dark water to reach the lifeboat. Still, despite chaotic and stressful circumstances, that bunch of blue-collar guys in pajamas followed the process that had been outlined. And they all survived.

Twenty minutes after impact, the four fishermen watched the boat, their belongings, and their paycheck slowly sink into the Atlantic.

No finger-pointing occurred as their life raft floated aimlessly in the current of a 3:30 a.m. July sea. No doubt, they would be saved at some point—it was just a matter of time, since the area was relatively heavily traveled by boats as well as cargo ships. In the end, they would have to wait six hours before being rescued by a crab trawler, which had noticed the flares they shot into the clear sky every 30 minutes.

Debris left behind by a cargo ship or a sunken log had probably caused the damage to the hull of the now-sunken Lancer. A month of upgrading the boat, $80,000 of labor, parts, tools, technology, and gear had been swallowed up in a moment, but all that could be repaid and re-earned. The only thing that mattered was that those on board lived to tell the tale and fish again. Make that three of the four fishermen fished again— the rookie never set foot on another fishing vessel, opting for a land job instead.

Ironically, although Dad would go on to captain the Andrea Gail in much rougher and riskier conditions in the deep waters of the North Atlantic 1,000-plus nautical miles away from Gloucester Harbor, that would be the only time he would ever have to abandon ship. Learning about the Lancer sinking in flat-calm waters not far from home taught me that you need to be prepared regardless of your location or your destination.

Strategic Preparation & Protection

Yes, sometimes, the boat sinks. Not every day is a good day to fish, and even when it is, horrific things can happen. But more often than not, by good fortune, skill, and the grace of God, Dad put fish on the boat, and lots of it, time and time again. He knew the risks he faced, and he made sure he was ready for the ones he could anticipate as well as the ones he couldn't.

Let's face it. The ocean is a vast territory with many unknowns. When the knowns don't work out, you have to go to Plan B, which you'll learn all about in this chapter as well as Chapter 7. For now, it's safe to say that Plan B is always stressful, uncomfortable, and potentially even riskier. On the other hand, if you never leave the dock, it doesn't matter if you have a vessel or not. You won't get anywhere. The answer to the safety versus risk quandary lies in the use of strategic preparation and protection when it comes to asset positioning. In the world of investing, that means being able to tap diverse financial instruments that will pay off in good times and bad.

At Beauport, we target 21 different asset classes—including value, growth, emerging markets, small- and mid-cap, dividend payors, natural resources, investment-grade bonds, and short-term corporate bonds—in a globally diversified portfolio for our investors' trust, retirement account, or traditional brokerage account. We do this in a tax-efficient and low-cost manner by utilizing ETFs. We like to call this *active indexing*. Buying an index is not a one-time, don't-look-back type of strategy. Unlike my dad and his crew, who were focused on targeting one specific species of fish, we like to put the baited hooks in various parts of the investment waters for yield dividends and returns from a variety of asset classes that perform differently.

This type of asset allocation strategy is designed to manage and mitigate the overall risk of an investment portfolio rather than aiming for a home run with any one stock or ETF position. Our goal is to generate a reasonable rate of return with less risk than the investment market bears. When people retire and move from earning money to tapping their investments in order to fund their new lifestyle, they're not exactly looking to place big bets with their asset base. They know that in all likelihood, no more contributions will be going into those accounts.

That's just the start. Asset positioning or asset location is just as important as asset allocation. Let's say you've got 70 percent of your funds allocated to stocks and 30 percent to bonds. "That sounds safe," you think to yourself. "My eggs are definitely not all in one basket." Of course, if that 70 percent that's invested in equities isn't correctly positioned in various stock sectors (such as energy, high tech, materials, healthcare, communications, etc.), you're not going to see the return you're hoping for. And if you've got them all in one sector, then you've still got more than two-thirds of your eggs in a single basket. That's why knowing where and how to locate your funds matters so much. The Grand Banks, where Dad fished for swords, is a vast area; his knowledge about where to position the boat, along with the equipment he would need to help locate the fish, was vital for a good harvest.

Annual Returns

2018	2019	2020	2021	2022	2023
U.S. Fixed Income 0.01%	Large Cap Equity 31.49%	Small Cap Equity 19.96%	Large Cap Equity 28.71%	High Yield -11.19%	Large Cap Equity 26.29%
High Yield -2.08%	Small Cap Equity 25.52%	Large Cap Equity 18.40%	Real Estate 26.09%	U.S. Fixed Income -13.01%	Dev ex-U.S. Equity 17.94%
Global ex-U.S. Fixed Income -2.15%	Dev ex-U.S. Equity 22.49%	Emerging Market Equity 18.31%	Small Cap Equity 14.82%	Dev ex-U.S. Equity -14.29%	Small Cap Equity 16.93%
Large Cap Equity -4.38%	Real Estate 21.91%	Global ex-U.S. Fixed Income 10.11%	Dev ex-U.S. Equity 12.62%	Large Cap Equity -18.11%	High Yield 13.44%
Real Estate -5.63%	Emerging Market Equity 18.44%	Dev ex-U.S. Equity 7.59%	High Yield 5.28%	Global ex-U.S. Fixed Income -18.70%	Emerging Market Equity 9.83%
Small Cap Equity -11.01%	High Yield 14.32%	U.S. Fixed Income 7.51%	U.S. Fixed Income -1.54%	Emerging Market Equity -20.09%	Real Estate 9.67%
Dev ex-U.S. Equity -14.09%	U.S. Fixed Income 8.72%	High Yield 7.11%	Emerging Market Equity -2.54%	Small Cap Equity -20.44%	Global ex-U.S. Fixed Income 5.72%
Emerging Market Equity -14.57%	Global ex-U.S. Fixed Income 5.09%	Real Estate -9.04%	Global ex-U.S. Fixed Income -7.05%	Real Estate -25.10%	U.S. Fixed Income 5.53%

Monthly Returns

Jan 2024	Feb 2024	Mar 2024	Apr 2024	May 2024	Jun 2024	YTD
Large Cap Equity 1.68%	Small Cap Equity 5.65%	Small Cap Equity 3.58%	Emerging Market Equity 0.45%	Small Cap Equity 5.02%	Emerging Market Equity 3.94%	Large Cap Equity 15.29%
Dev ex-U.S. Equity 0.43%	Large Cap Equity 5.34%	Real Estate 3.45%	High Yield -0.94%	Large Cap Equity 4.96%	Large Cap Equity 3.59%	Emerging Market Equity 7.49%
High Yield 0.00%	Emerging Market Equity 4.76%	Dev ex-U.S. Equity 3.37%	U.S. Fixed Income -2.53%	Dev ex-U.S. Equity 3.82%	U.S. Fixed Income 0.95%	Dev ex-U.S. Equity 4.96%
U.S. Fixed Income -0.27%	Dev ex-U.S. Equity 1.71%	Large Cap Equity 3.22%	Global ex-U.S. Fixed Income -2.59%	Real Estate 3.41%	High Yield 0.94%	High Yield 2.58%
Global ex-U.S. Fixed Income -2.29%	High Yield 0.29%	Emerging Market Equity 2.48%	Dev ex-U.S. Equity -2.65%	U.S. Fixed Income 1.70%	Real Estate 0.34%	Small Cap Equity 1.73%
Small Cap Equity -3.89%	Real Estate -0.60%	High Yield 1.18%	Large Cap Equity -4.08%	High Yield 1.10%	Global ex-U.S. Fixed Income -0.51%	U.S. Fixed Income -0.71%
Real Estate -4.02%	Global ex-U.S. Fixed Income -1.18%	U.S. Fixed Income 0.92%	Real Estate -6.97%	Global ex-U.S. Fixed Income 1.00%	Small Cap Equity -0.93%	Real Estate -3.70%
Emerging Market Equity -4.64%	U.S. Fixed Income -1.41%	Global ex-U.S. Fixed Income 0.24%	Small Cap Equity -7.04%	Emerging Market Equity 0.56%	Dev ex-U.S. Equity -1.66%	Global ex-U.S. Fixed Income -5.26%

Sources: ● Bloomberg Aggregate ● Bloomberg Corp High Yield ● Bloomberg Global Aggregate ex US ● FTSE EPRA Nareit Developed ● MSCI Emerging Markets ● MSCI World ex USA ● Russell 2000 ● S&P 500

Asset positioning starts with a targeted design and an IPS (Investment Policy Statement) that sets the course and parameters. The design, implementation, and management of the portfolio are just as crucial as the rebalancing and monitoring of the treasure. Markets change as do tax laws, so maintenance and management are vital. Just as it's easy to drift off course at sea, for example, it's easy to start with a 70-30 portfolio of stocks and bonds and find yourself in an 80-20 position after a big run-up in the stock market. You then either correct your course or decide to alter your course on purpose. And no matter how well you're doing, you make sure you have a fallback plan.

The fact is that you have to be prepared for the storms of life as well as unexpected events in the global financial marketplace. Realizing after the fact that you're off course is anxiety-filled and counterproductive. Conversely, planning considerations and conversations ahead of expected events are prudent. If you haven't considered how you would handle a significant market decline or an elongated recession ahead of such an event, it's high time to do so now. You must have a game plan that will ensure that you have the financial resources you need to cover your lifestyle expenses without having to sell investments at a loss.

As we've seen, since 1950, the average U.S. recession historically has lasted about 10 months. Since recessions occur on average every six-and-a-half years, you have to be prepared for that reality with cash reserves and a reliable stream of income to fund your retirement lifestyle.

When you are retired and drawing down income from your nest egg, you should have six to twelve months of spending needs in a money market or cash account for obvious safety reasons. Just to be prudent, another year of budget capital should be allocated to shorter-term government bonds.

To avoid the risk of a "broker" fishing trip and to provide confidence in the journey called retirement, you can also create a personal pension by taking a portion of your savings and investing in an annuity to receive future income payments. Let me explain.

Get a GRIP! Guaranteed Retirement Income Program

As you probably know all too well, private pensions provided by employers are harder and harder to find these days if you're working in the private sector. According to the U.S. Bureau of Labor Statistics, only 15 percent of U.S. companies offer a retiree a pension. However, you can establish your own guaranteed retirement income program (GRIP) by investing a portion of the assets you've earmarked for retirement into an income annuity. As annuities are tied to insurance companies, any guarantee is limited to the claims-paying ability of the issuing carrier.

Here's how this transfer of income risk concept works. You give the annuity carrier a certain amount of capital, and you get a fixed amount credited to the income rider no matter what happens. If you need $5,000 a month to live, and you're only getting $3,000 from Social Security and other investments, that extra $2,000 a month to reach the goal of $5,000 is money you can't have at risk. By transferring the necessary capital to an annuity, as an investor, you can have confidence when the market fluctuates, because you know that your annuity is designed to fill that income gap.

Let's look at this another way. Let's say you have $1.5 million in an IRA. By carving off $500,000 of that amount and investing it in a variable annuity, two things will be put into motion:

1. Assuming that the annuity contains a 5 percent income benefit rider, that $500,000 asset will generate $25,000 a year or more in income even during a market decline, theoretically allowing you to leave the rest of your portfolio untouched until the market rebounds and prices eventually come back up in your portfolio. That means you will have better staying power when market fluctuations happen.

2. You have an income stream that is designed to last for life, and you could receive a raise if your portfolio outperforms the income guarantee.

Think of GRIP as your retirement lifestyle insurance plan. By transferring the risk from you to the insurance company backing the annuity, a GRIP by definition—and contract—is designed for you to receive an income stream for your lifetime, regardless of how the underlying fund account performs assuming there is always at least $1 in the account.

Now, this income rider comes at a cost. With the income assurance, your return may not be as much as it might have been had you been invested in the market, but you could also make less with just a traditional investment portfolio and not have that income assurance, or even lose your investment entirely. As a general rule, if you are over 65, you should expect a 5 percent payout from your income annuity, for life, which translates to $5,000 annually per $100,000 invested.

In an investment portfolio, risk is inexpensive and guarantees cost more, so this GRIP strategy is likely to be pricier than what you're used to when it comes to associated fees. While a managed IRA generally carries a 1 to 1.5 percent advisory fee, the fees related to managing and implementing the more complicated GRIP strategy usually run in the 2.5 to 3.25 percent a year range. However, the more inexpensively run IRA portfolio cannot guarantee an income for life, and once it runs dry, the money and the revenue are gone. A GRIP strategy, though more expensive to manage and implement, provides income assurances that a specific lifestyle budget can be maintained.

If there's one thing we learned from the 2008 Great Recession, it's that in addition to having cash in reserve, we need a stream of guaranteed income for those days when the fishing isn't looking so bright or danger strikes. On the high seas, everyone needs to know where the life raft is, where the auto emergency beacon is, where the survival suit is and how to get into it. You need that same kind of dependable process that addresses the reliability and predictability of income planning in smooth seas as well as in rough storms. When it's no longer a rehearsal and everything is going south, you need to know what to do next. And no matter how bad things get, you need to know that it will all be okay.

That's what worked for Gretchen. The retiree, who had diligently saved her money during the decades she worked at Gorton's of Gloucester, was finally doing the traveling and exploring she had always dreamed of. She looked forward to each new adventure—be it a cruise to Alaska, a California wine country experience, or a European sightseeing tour—that would allow her to see the world firsthand in the company of friends.

Gretchen was getting ready to head to Alaska on a much-anticipated luxury cruise and needed $5,000 to finalize payment when the 2008 domestic and global stock markets were spiraling downward. Most of the time, the last thing you want to do in a down market is sell, thereby making paper losses real. But we didn't need to. Instead, we used her annual income assurances from an income annuity and left her managed portfolio alone since prices continued to fall in the investment markets.

This type of risk management strategy is like an income lifeboat. Just knowing that you have a way to access additional funds to finance your retirement needs or desires without selling your other investments can provide peace of mind. No one can predict all the storms or their duration. For that matter, as my dad can tell you, no one can predict those unforeseen calamities when things unexpectedly go bump in the night. As a result, it's essential to have a process and a contingency plan in place, which we'll talk about even more in the chapter called "Steaming Back Home & Taking Stock." The transfer of income risk allows you to use income annuities when needed to supplement other guaranteed income sources like government pensions and Social Security while, regardless of the economic climate, continuing to enjoy the fruit of hard-earned seeds planted a long time ago.

Trading investment risk and all that related anxiety for built-in protection means a lot more than sweating the extra fees associated with transferring risk as opposed to managing risk.

Here's the one potential catch. Contingency planning must be done before water is flooding your financial ship, and before the economic winds are howling and you can no longer see straight. Have these discussions with your planner when the markets are calm, and profits are up. Then put your GRIP in place without delay, before you need it, so you know you'll be safe.

My dad didn't have that luxury. When it was time to abandon ship, he had to jump into the sea and swim for the lifeboat. Thankfully, when it comes to your financial assets, you can take a much different and more measured approach. That starts with establishing a protocol for what to do when things get rough, not unlike a boat's crew knowing exactly where the survival suits are located, how to put them on, and how to deploy the life rafts. It also involves regular check-ups. You need to make sure not only that your Plan B will take care of you in case of an emergency, but that your financial ship is in good working order.

Financial Checkups

Just as the 40-year-old looking to get to a certain accumulation number for retirement in 25 years needs to chart an investing course that will grow their assets regardless of what the future holds, which we'll discuss in more detail in Chapter 6, the retiree needs to chart an investing course that will see them through their golden years. This kind of income planning is critical when it comes to creating a reliable, steady, and growing personal income stream for your retirement years—regardless of the catch or market conditions.

We still aren't aware of all that is in the deep blue ocean as we cannot see it all below the waterline, but with a little knowledge, research, prudence, and perspective, one can seek treasure while avoiding the iceberg. On the other hand, you want to make sure you have a viable Plan B in place at all times. That means having your financial plan assessed annually.

If you think about it, that makes total sense. You go to the doctor for physical maintenance, to the dentist for oral care, and to the mechanic for auto upkeep. You may even hire landscapers and contractors for property management. But how often are you revising and assessing your finances to keep them in good efficient order?

Taking care of your financial ship means putting it in dry dock at least once a year, so it gets taken out of the water for a full inspection. Letting a professional give your financial ship a once-over and make any necessary tweaks or repairs to get it in prime condition is the only way to ensure it's seaworthy.

Will this annual review entail some effort and expense on your part? Sure. But this is your livelihood we are talking about. Just as storms brewing in the Gulf or Caribbean affect fishing in the Grand Banks and so must be taken into account, you want to be well prepared for any upcoming financial storms and adjust your course and your allocation accordingly.

There will still be plenty of surprises in life and in the markets, just as there are on the water. But at least you'll know what's on the radar. And with the help of your financial advisor, you'll have that Plan B in place for when the unexpected throws a severe kink into Plan A. That's why you want to work with a comprehensive planner who isn't just looking at your assets in a vacuum, not knowing what other advice, accounts, or plans are in place.

Planning, risk protection strategies, and management of your wealth should be part of the same holistic conversation that you, your family, and your tax and legal advisors are all familiar with. At Beauport Financial, for example, we do not consider ourselves to be money managers or stock pickers. Instead, our firm advocates for our clients in the vast financial marketplace, and we serve as financial quarterbacks (or financial captains) for them. We construct targeted asset-allocated portfolios, mitigate risk, and design income plans for retirees that can grow and protect what is theirs.

Capitalizing on Opportunity
After having to abandon ship, Dad was back fishing within weeks despite his firsthand lesson that boats don't just sink when the seas are rough, but also in flat, calm water. However, staying afloat wasn't the only risk he ran. Even when weather or underwater hazards weren't an issue, there was always the chance that a trip wouldn't pay off, a story you'll read about in Chapter 7. But the ocean and its bountiful treasure proved irresistible. Besides, he knew that

where there's risk, there's opportunity. And when the opportunity hits, bonanza!

Several years after the ill-fated Lancer trip, Dad got a fax on the Andrea Gail showing a new swordfishing spot. The faxed images at that time noted water depths and temperatures, and both seemed optimum, about 10 degrees warmer than the surrounding water and so an ideal place for the swords as they seek food. He noticed seaweed and seagrass floating on top of the water, along with a swirling current (otherwise known as an eddy) below the waterline, which he knew meant plentiful cold-water baitfish, which would draw the swordfish who feed on them.

Dad had never fished this spot, so it was a risk. But he couldn't discount the signs, so he followed his instincts. And wow, was he ever right! Five nights of fishing in the eddy swirling south-southwest of Labrador Current and Grand Banks, the area that Dad typically headed toward, yielded 38,000 pounds of fish. Talk about a honey spot.

He would have loved to stay and keep harvesting those fish that were almost throwing themselves in the boat. Instead, because of fuel levels, he adapted the plan, stopped early, and headed home. The 15-day trip added $17,000 to our household funds.

That kind of good bounty earned the captain the praise of the "old salts," who had hung up their fishing slickers, as well as the respect of the crew who beat him to the local bar for a few pops. Then he came home so we could celebrate the way we always did—with a family dinner at the Millstone Restaurant in Ipswich. We would have plenty of canned-tuna-casserole nights ahead when the month's catch didn't live up to expectations, but this time the risk had paid off.

Strategic Risk-Taking
Whether fishing for swordfish or investment returns, you must be able to capitalize on opportunity. In financial terms, this means making sure your assets are working for you so that if the market is up 20 percent, you're participating rather than putting money in after the fact because you were "safely" asleep at the dock instead of out fishing.

> *I find the great in this world is not so much where we stand, as in what direction we are moving: To reach the port of heaven, we must sail sometimes with the wind and sometimes against it, but we must sail, and not drift, nor lie at anchor.*
>
> – Oliver Wendell Holmes,
> *The Autocrat of the Breakfast-Table*, 1891

As humans, we are conditioned to avoid risk and seek pleasure rather than pain. But we need to strategically battle that tendency when it comes to saving for retirement. Sure, it's a bit painful to save and invest part of every paycheck as you go along the journey of life, especially when that entails taking calculated risks. But if you modestly invest in a bigger, better future, you can mitigate that risk.

The key is to start saving and investing early. That way, you don't have to go for broke or hit a home run. Trying to play catch up is what gets us in trouble because that increases the risk. When you push too hard, bad things occur more often than when you don't.

What's too hard?

The answer to that question is different for each of us and depends as much on assets as personality. You need to have a conversation about risk with the captain of your financial ship. Before that transpires, ask yourself:

- What is your risk tolerance regarding your finances and your financial situation?
- Are you aware of the risks out there, and have you identified them?

Dad, by nature, was not a risk-taker, but he had to support his family, so he did what he needed to do, which meant spending a good part of his life in peril. As I've mentioned, from weather conditions and a work environment replete with knives, hooks, and the catch itself—with its five-to-ten-foot-long sword sharp enough to slash and injure its prey—thrashing around on deck, risk abounded. On the financial side of things, with all the money spent on gear, boat upkeep, technology, and tools for the ship, to say nothing of insurance, fuel, engine maintenance, etc., nobody was ever guaranteed a paycheck. Not the boat owner, not the captain, and certainly not the crew. One could leave the dock for a month at a time and return empty-handed when it came to both fish and money. So, the job came with its fair (or unfair) share of stress. Would you be the boisterous big shot at the bar buying rounds of drinks for others, or quietly heading home from the dock, cigarette in your mouth, duffel bag of dirty clothes on your shoulder, and a sullen look on your face knowing that the investment of time, energy, and stress hadn't paid off this month, but the everyday living expenses would continue?

On the other hand, Dad knew the fish were out there, so he made sure he had a good boat, a solid crew, and a game plan in both cases of scarcity and abundance.

Do you have those game plans in place? If not, it's time for you to talk to your planner and make sure that your navigation plan for the last and arguably most important financial voyage of your existence is as comprehensive as it needs to be. The only certainties you can count on are that both calm and rough seas lie ahead, that fish (as well as investments) move, and that currents and weather change. Your plan must be able to adapt to the shifting landscape of markets, taxes, and any other relevant information that will impact your investments or how you live your life. You will enjoy many adventures in retirement, and the last thing you may want to concern yourself with on a Tuscan-wine vacation is how the markets are reacting to rising interest rates or whatever. Confidence comes from knowing you're safe and comfortable regardless of external financial conditions, and the resources will not run dry.

Assessing your Appetite and Need for Risk
When it comes to investing, your game plan on either front starts with determining how much risk you need to take to meet your retirement goals and whether your appetite for risk is big or small.

RISK TOLERANCE QUESTIONNAIRE

This questionnaire is designed to identify the appropriate asset allocation that is best suited for your investment. The following questions are split into two categories: **TIME HORIZON** and **RISK TOLERANCE**. These questions consider your goals, investment experience, and attitude toward market risk. Please check the box that best describes you and total the corresponding values in the respective "SCORE" field.

TIME HORIZON

Check the box for the number of points for each of your answers to get your total TIME HORIZON score.

1. My Current Age Is:

< 50 Years	☐ 10
50–55 Years	☐ 8
56–62 Years	☐ 5
63–69 Years	☐ 4
≥ 70 Years	☐ 2

2. I Plan on Starting to Make Withdrawals on My Investment In:

≥ 15 Years	☐ 10
10–14 Years	☐ 8
7–9 Years	☐ 5
4–6 Years	☐ 3
≤ 3 Years	☐ 0

3. I Plan on Depleting My Investment In:

> 25 Years	☐ 8
16–25 Years	☐ 5
11–15 Years	☐ 3
6–10 Years	☐ 1
≤ 5 Years	☐ 0

Results:

2–9 Pts	Short
10–15 Pts	Limited
16–22 Pts	Moderate
23–28 Pts	Long

Enter the total points from questions 1–3.

TIME HORIZON SCORE: _____

RISK TOLERANCE

Check the box for the number of points you got for each of your answers to get your **RISK TOLERANCE** score.

4. The Percentage of My Overall Investible Assets That This Account Represents Is:

< 25%	☐ 6
25–50%	☐ 4
51–75%	☐ 2
> 75%	☐ 1

5. My Overall Knowledge of Investments Is:

Extensive	☐ 8
Good	☐ 5
Limited	☐ 3
None	☐ 2

6. When Thinking About My Investment, I Would Describe Myself As:

Wanting aggressive growth potential with large fluctuation in value.	☐ 8
Wanting moderate growth potential with reasonable fluctuation in value.	☐ 5
Wanting limited growth potential with small fluctuation in value.	☐ 1

RISK TOLERANCE QUESTIONNAIRE

7. If the Value of My Investment Decreased By 20% In One Year, I Would Most Likely:

Have no concern of my investment loss, thinking of ways to buy more of this investment.	☐ 8
Have some concern of my investment loss, wondering if I should sell low or buy the dip.	☐ 5
Have a large concern of my investment loss, selling my investment immediately.	☐ 1

8. Look at the Following Worst/Best Case Scenarios. Which Range of Outcomes Is Most Acceptable to You?

	Plan	Average Annual Return	Best-Case Return	Worst-Case Return	Points
☐	A	5.6%	14.4%	-3.4%	1
☐	B	9.1%	24.0%	-11.9%	3
☐	C	10.2%	31.4%	-19.4%	5
☐	D	11.8%	41.7%	-23.7%	8
☐	E	12.8%	50.0%	-31.2%	10

Enter the total points from questions 4–8.
RISK TOLERANCE SCORE: _____

INTERPRETING YOUR RESULTS

Using your **TIME HORIZON** score (Long, Moderate, Limited, Short) and your **RISK TOLERANCE** score (6–40), find the intersection on either the visual or numeric plot below to identify the appropriate asset allocation best suited for your investment. On the next page, select the investment strategy that corresponds to your results.

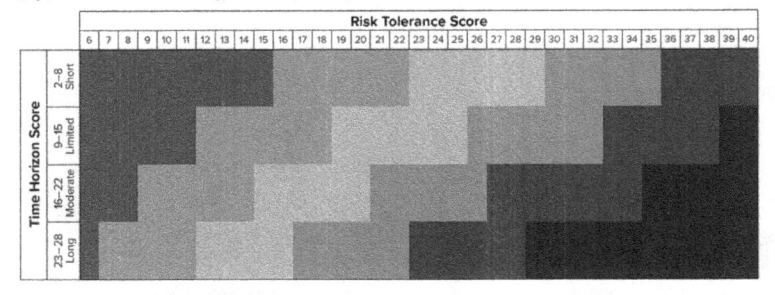

	Conservative	Income & Growth	Balanced	Moderate Growth	Growth	Aggressive Growth
Short	<16	16–22	23–29	30–35	36–40	–
Limited	<12	12–18	19–25	26–32	33–38	39–40
Moderate	<9	9–14	15–20	21–26	27–34	35–40
Long	<7	7–11	12–16	17–22	23–28	29–40

RISK TOLERANCE QUESTIONNAIRE

SELECT AN INVESTMENT STRATEGY

If one of the investment strategies below matches the combination of your **RISK TOLERANCE** and **TIME HORIZON** scores, you can use this information to help you create an asset allocation plan. Please note that it is important to periodically review your investment strategy to make sure it continues to be consistent with your goals.

Conservative
Appropriate for investors seeking an investment to provide primarily income, with growth of capital and a relatively low level of volatility.

Income and Growth
Appropriate for investors seeking an investment to provide primarily income, with growth of capital and a relatively low level of volatility.

Balanced
Appropriate for investors seeking an investment to provide a total return in the form of capital and income, while maintaining a moderate level of volatility.

Moderate Growth
Appropriate for investors seeking an investment to provide growth of capital, where capital growth takes precedence over the reduction of volatility.

Growth
Appropriate for investors seeking an investment to provide primarily growth of capital, at a level of risk expected to be lower than that of an investor fully invested in equity-based investment options. This portfolio allocates some investments to bonds and money market assets in order to diversify and reduce volatility.

Aggressive Growth
Appropriate for investors seeking an investment to provide primarily growth of capital through investments across multiple equity asset classes. The portfolio is anticipated to be the riskiest available, thus clients invested in this portfolio should expect greater volatility and more aggressive risk/return characteristics.

- Total U.S. Stock Market
- Extended U.S. Stock Market
- International Developed
- Emerging Markets
- Natural Resources
- Cash
- Core Bond
- TIPS
- High Yield Bond

Chapter 4

To determine your risk tolerance, you'll want to explore some fundamental questions on your own and with your financial planner. Check out the investment risk tolerance chart below.

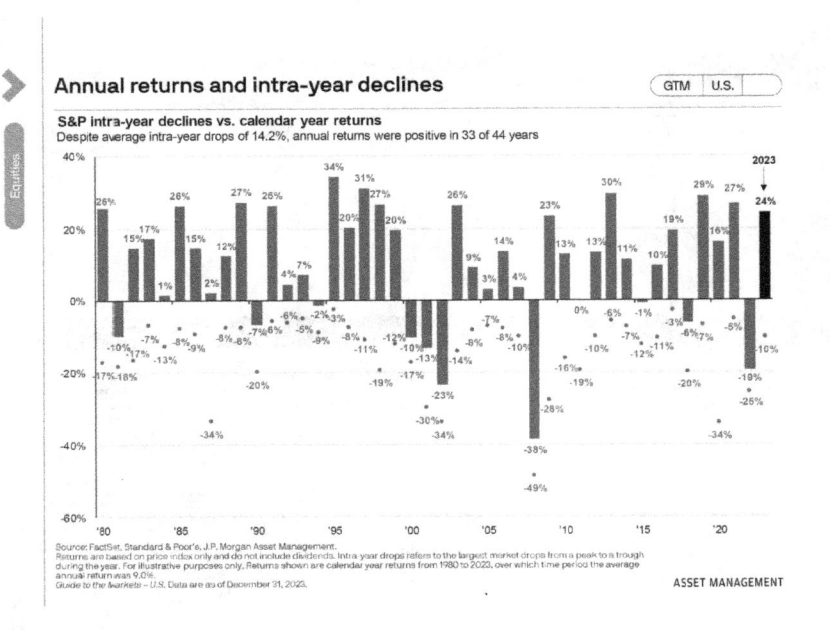

Annual returns and intra-year declines — GTM U.S.

S&P intra-year declines vs. calendar year returns
Despite average intra-year drops of 14.2%, annual returns were positive in 33 of 44 years

Source: FactSet, Standard & Poor's, J.P. Morgan Asset Management.
Returns are based on price index only and do not include dividends. Intra-year drops refers to the largest market drops from a peak to a trough during the year. For illustrative purposes only. Returns shown are calendar year returns from 1980 to 2022, over which time period the average annual return was 9.0%.
Guide to the Markets – U.S. Data are as of December 31, 2023.

ASSET MANAGEMENT

To determine how well you're strategically positioned for the next time the market crashes (and trust me, it will), ask your planner:

- **Do we have a process when it comes to my investments?** Most of the time, the answer will be no. That's because you've likely never had that conversation about risk we talked about earlier. I also ask newer investors and clients if their $1 million drops to $900,000 before it goes to $1.1 million—or loses 10 percent of its value before gaining

10 percent—whether they'll lose sleep. Or can they trust the process and reinvest dividends and funds in a temporary down market, knowing the tide eventually comes back in and they'll be rewarded

Once you ascertain your risk tolerance, you also need to ask:

- **Will I be okay if things go south?**
  If the response is yes, you'll want to know what that answer is based on. If the response is no, you and your planner (or perhaps the new one you hire) have some quick work to do.

In 2008, my partner at Beauport Financial and I learned first and foremost that you absolutely have to have a game plan when dealing with a perfect storm of financial chaos.

Luckily that kind of perfect storm seldom occurs. At the time, however, most of our clients told us that although they were scared about what was happening with the financial markets, they were reassured that they were not 100 percent invested in any one asset class and had set aside enough living expenses to get them through such a situation. They just wanted to go to the mailbox and find that monthly $5,000 check that would supplement Social Security and their pension.

That's why solely having a stockbroker, insurance broker, or money manager is not going to cut it. You should seek a highly competent financial planning professional just as you would seek a qualified estate tax planner to make sense of your entire estate, along with a CPA to advise you on your overall tax preparations. A planner uses various processes and instruments to look at what's right in front of them as well as what's lurking over the horizon. Then, true to their name, they make a plan that assesses risk vs. volatility.

I'll explain using, as always, the swordfishing analogy. Volatility means knowing that the weather is going to get worse, and the winds and seas will pick up, but you have the capability to handle what's coming and see it through. Risk is making the judgment call about whether to stay out at sea for one more haul in order to fill the hold or, instead, to head for home. If the storm hits, then you have to decide whether heading into or away from it is the best call.

While risk can be mitigated, volatility is ever-present, a fact you must accept before you even leave the dock. Boats were designed and intended to be launched and then captained with great purpose, but the very same seas that give opportunity also present risks that must be contended with and managed.

As an investor, both volatility swings and risk can be your friend. The convergence of dangerous conditions responsible for the financial perfect storm that ruined so many people's lives actually benefitted others. Over time, lots of money can be made by investing in volatility, since that means buying more shares of stock or bonds at lower prices. Once the market recovers, you're in better shape than before simply because you have more shares than you started with, all valued at the market's higher prices.

Good financial captains practice risk mitigation through, among other things, a globally diversified portfolio. Essentially that boils down to, like a squirrel, not stashing your cache—or in this case your investments—in one single place. While you want to buy mostly stocks during the accumulation phase to reach your number, for example, you don't just want stocks. You want bonds as well since they're traditionally less volatile than stocks. You don't want to only buy Apple stock, because if Apple takes a nosedive, you lose in a huge way. When it comes to asset allocation, you're looking to put together a portfolio of different types of sectors and companies—some that pay dividends and others that don't—that don't all move in concert with one another. That's the traditional, wise, and prudent investment strategy, which is dictated by your investment policy statement (IPS).

In 2002–2003, and again following 2008–2009, we onboarded a number of family and business clients after they had lost a lot of money because their portfolios were over-weighted in tech and the dot.com stocks. As a result, they got stuck selling on the way down, which is never fun. They realized after the fact that while they had investment accounts of a certain high value, no real financial plan or attention had addressed risk mitigation, income planning, or proper asset positioning.

Good financial captains consistently measure the risks that need to be taken against the reward that can be earned. Like Dad, they know that not every day is a day for fishing. As I mentioned earlier, you have to understand when to steam out or stay put, when to have the lines in the water, and when to haul them in and head for home. Financial planners who know their stuff don't shoot for the moon. They know you don't need the market's top stocks. You just need the ones that will provide you with the rate of return you require and no more.

In that way, reliable financial planners minimize the risk you run. If you are seeking 6 to 7 percent returns in a balanced portfolio, then you just defined where to place your assets and set your expectations—fish in those waters for assurances. And when the market dips before it soars, have faith in the numbers and the plan. You might even want to buy more with additional cash.

Yes, sometimes investing is about preservation and protection. But unless you know what kinds of risks you're running into, you can't make any kind of informed decisions about what to do. Let's look at six types of risks retirees run when it comes to money and what they mean.

Six Risk Factors that Require Attention

The following list of risks is worth paying attention to. This isn't just your money we're talking about; it's how well you're going to be able to live your life. So, heads up!

Here are the six risk factors that you and your financial planner need to discuss in terms of financial management strategy:

1. **Liquidity**—The risk that when life's unexpected financial events happen, you will have flexibility to access your funds. The need for flexibility is paramount when that earned-income check has stopped coming in, and you're now relying on income distribution from your assets. It's important to be able to access enough capital not tied up with financial instruments that have a fee or penalty attached.
2. **Longevity**—The risk that you will outlive your money. Retirees used to be more concerned with dying too soon

and not enjoying the spoils of hard-earned savings and the sacrifices they made to finance their retirement. As medicine, technology, and mortality all advance, however, you potentially need financial resources for three decades in retirement.

3. **Market Sequence of Return**—The risk that early on in retirement when you are relying on an income stream from your asset base, the invested portfolio drops significantly. Equities have proven to be an excellent long-term wealth creator and a hedge against inflation even in retirement years. While a dramatic drop in the stock market causes paper losses on your portfolio, those can be compounded and made "real" with ill-timed distributions to support your retirement lifestyle. You know by now that the average recession lasts about 10 months. Having a year or so of income in financial reserves or a way to meet your income needs during that time will protect you from having to sell at the low.

4. **Inflation**—The guaranteed risk that the costs of things will go up. An income portfolio has to address cost of living adjustments and tax implications on the gross amounts earmarked for retirement income, especially when it comes to healthcare, medicine, food, energy, goods, and services.

5. **Health**—The risk that long-term health care expenses will wreak havoc on your retirement nest egg. The national average cost of long-term health care each month is approaching $10,000, according to a 2023 Genworth survey. There has to be a conversation about how this high-percentage reality is going to be handled both financially and practically from a caregiver perspective.

6. **Survivor**—The risk of leaving behind a financial obligation on those you love. The last kind of legacy you want is one that's a financial burden on your heirs. If debt will be left behind once you're gone, be sure there are clear means for income or assets to address it.

Mitigating Risk

There are three ways to address risk when it comes to investing. You can:

- Avoid risk with cash or CDs, a pension, or Social Security.
- Manage risk with custom-built ETFs and actively managed fund portfolios.
- Transfer the income risk with variable annuities and/or cash-value life insurance programs. As we saw above, that's how Gretchen was able to take that luxury cruise in 2009 when so many other people were hoarding their pennies and counting their losses.

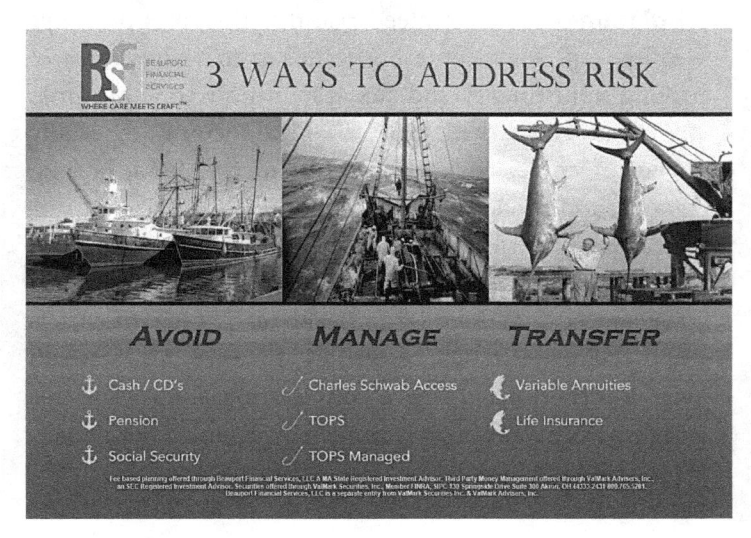

3 WAYS TO ADDRESS RISK

Avoid	Manage	Transfer
Cash / CD's	Charles Schwab Access	Variable Annuities
Pension	TOPS	Life Insurance
Social Security	TOPS Managed	

Mitigating risk with the right process—one that incorporates various planning scenarios, the right crew, and the right instruments—means setting a course through high seas, calm waters, and everything in between.

What's Your Process?

You and your financial planner need to come up with an investment policy statement that determines:

- How much money is going to be at risk in the stock market,
- How much will be at lower risk with fixed income or bonds,
- Whether (and how) you're going to transfer risk in return for a guaranteed monthly amount of money.

A good planner will listen to your concerns and revise recommendations as appropriate.

As we've seen, while there is ever-present risk to be avoided, managed, and even transferred, opportunity also abounds. So even if your investment policy statement says that half your investments should be in bonds, for example, it's up to you and your advisor to discuss which bonds to include. A general recipe is not good enough. When it comes to both asset allocation (how your funds are divvied up) and asset location or positioning (where you're investing), your financial captain must provide specific details based on conditions and needs.

As good financial captains, we don't just try certain things, and if they don't work out, then, ho-hum, we sell and put your money somewhere else. Smart fishermen don't go just anywhere in the vast blue sea and cast a line, but instead rely on institutional and common knowledge, history and experience, charts, currents, and water temps. You have to fish where the fish are or will be, or you'll get shut out. Similarly, in our business, we rely on historical, reliable, dividend-paying companies, as well as growth-focused companies, income-generating bonds, and annuities.

(Of course, the artistry comes in when, despite all the signs screaming for you to head to the habitual fishing grounds and set your hooks, your gut compels you to do something else, and you wind up being right. However, just like Dad who sure didn't depend on being lucky when it came to catching swords or returning home safely, we're never going to risk big chunks of people's retirement on a hunch. We're going to use our analytical skills, expertise, and investment tools to help our clients grow their investments in the best way we know how. And that doesn't necessarily mean following the crowd.)

Implementing the Financial Planning Recommendations

Once you and the financial planner agree that the plan is prudent, justified, and in the best interest of all concerned, it's time to push off from the dock. Of course, someone will still always need to be on the alert regarding the implementation of the plan and/or the process since, as we've seen, even when the seas seem perfect, something can crop up that could potentially sink a ship or ruin an otherwise good trip.

The planner may carry out the recommendations or serve as a coach, coordinating the process with you and/or other professionals such as attorneys or stockbrokers. Either way, the goal is to make sure that your plan is sound and that the risks inherent in investing have been addressed.

This reminds me of a story about clients of ours, Bob and Kathleen. They were on holiday in Italy with another couple at the time when Greece was going bankrupt with no guarantee that the European Union would bail them out. At the same time, China contagion concerns were also causing massive fluctuations in both the domestic and global stock markets, with most of the wild ride plunging downward. As the market volatility ramped up, so did the media coverage.

As the reporting intensified, Bob and Kathleen's friends started to check their phones multiple times a day instead of immersing themselves in the amazing experience abroad.

"What's up?" Bob asked.

"The stock markets are selling off. Aren't you worried?"

"No, not really. We've got a game plan in place and professionals are looking after things for us, even when we're away," Kathleen replied calmly. "That's why we work with a planning firm—so we can enjoy our vacations."

Upon returning to the U.S., the anxious couple asked Kathleen and Bob for an introduction to Beauport. Those folks became long-term clients of ours and are now enjoying retirement with a little less stress, a lot more peace of mind, and a great wealth plan for their journey.

If you don't have a game plan that works this way, it's time to make that happen so that you, too, can rest easier.

Of course, there will always be risk when investing. But the most significant risk of all is one you can control. That's next.

CATCH OF THE DAY:

- Always stay diversified—utilize multiple asset classes, don't only chase returns—and rebalance annually according to your asset positioning. Your Investment Policy Statement defines how you care to be allocated, so stick to it or update it. The latest shiny object usually loses its luster and eventually fades. Staying invested and keeping the hooks in the water has provided investors with lots of treasure over the years.
- Plan for both the good and the challenging times. After an above-average year, pay down debt, make a gift, spend more if that's what you want to do, or set aside a higher amount in cash for a future financial storm. Pundits are always trying to predict the next move, as if they have a crystal ball. Please don't let the media or emotions dictate your financial success and happiness—the plan determines your course of action.

- Revisit your plan in both the good and the challenging times, never getting too elated in the plus years nor too disheartened in the down years. Trust your plan and your planner.
- Avoid risking investment capital to satisfy near-term income needs. Transfer your needed income risk as much as you can, and manage investment risk with an eye toward capital appreciation and your income goals for retirement. Creating monthly guaranteed income means creating peace of mind for yourself.

CHAPTER 5
IF YOU DON'T STAND FOR SOMETHING, YOU FALL FOR ANYTHING

"We're killing it!" Captain Ricky told my father. "Come on down."

With not much going on, Captain Charlie had decided to try to bring in one last haul before making the seasonal switch to groundfishing for cod, haddock, and flounder, which did not provide remotely the same level of compensation as that of a successful swordfishing trip. So, even though this had not been the plan, he had headed up north to Georges Bank at the Canadian border. The water temperature, however, had already dropped under that perfect 67-degree mark, and the only fish they found on the end of their hooks were sharks.

His buddy's news about the fishing bonanza down south helped quell the frustration that had been steadily mounting since arriving at the current fishing spot. The decision regarding what to do next seemed like a no-brainer. Dad turned the boat around and for two-plus days steamed toward the Virginia coast. By the time he arrived, however, more than a dozen boats had beaten him there.

Protocol dictates that the boats line up from east to west, which meant that he wound up toward the end of the line, west of those ideal conditions that had attracted all the swordfish. If you're a fisherman, there's little more irritating than knowing that other boats are raking in the cash and you're not catching a thing because you didn't get there quickly enough. The crew was not exactly pleased. From the captain's chair in the pilothouse, he could hear them complaining in the galley. He tried his best not to let that get to him, but it did. They were in this together. They depended on him to find the fish; then they'd get it on the boat. And he hadn't.

When it became clear that no amount of waiting around was going to improve the situation, Dad left the Virginia coast and headed to Hudson Canyon off the New York coast, where another friend was catching tuna. By the time they arrived, not many of those were left either.

Finally, after 20 days of chasing fish, only five of which were spent actually fishing, he returned home with very little to show for all that effort except for a lot of wasted gas and high frustration all around.

Fortunately, that didn't happen often to Dad. So why had this trip gone so poorly when he usually did so well? Two notable things: First, he didn't stick with his usual process. He had time to kill on this final trip of the fishing season, so he just went for it. Second, he didn't have a contingency game plan if the northern water temps weren't just right. Instead of being clear about his goal and his process, he let others' successes sway him. He and his crew paid the price since fishermen don't exactly make any money after a disappointing trip once all the expenses have been deducted.

"We would have been better off flipping burgers at McDonald's for minimum wage," he recalled when I interviewed him about that "broker" trip.

Some investors regularly do what Dad did on that trip. And yes, sometimes they get lucky. But here's the problem with chasing returns or going for the next shiny investment idea being promoted by whatever media. More often than not, you wind up chasing instead of hauling in the fish.

Of course, staying the course and not letting yourself be influenced isn't the easiest thing to do when everyone is voicing an opinion the moment you turn on your phone, computer, TV, open a newspaper, or buy a magazine.

Here's how reliable the news media is. In 2008, financial and economic commentators on TV, along with many politicos with access to a microphone and a camera, claimed that everything was fine with the banks, the housing market, and the mortgage business. This included high-ranking officials in the know, so to speak, among them the chair of the Federal Reserve, the Treasury secretary, the president, the two senators running for president at the time, the two chairmen of the Housing Committee, and many others on the inside who supposedly knew more than most.

"We're in the eighth inning of a bad ballgame—it's almost over," they claimed.

As it turned out, the ballgame was just getting started, and it was going to be an ugly event.

Were all those folks just lying to anyone listening in an attempt to minimize the impact of the financial storm that was about to be unleashed? Or did they really not know how bad things were about to get?

I'm not sure which is more damning—the deceit or the ignorance.

Having a front-row seat during the worst economic crisis that most folks have experienced in their lifetime was challenging to say the least. Investors were anxious, nervous, helpless, and unsure that there would be enough leadership and smarts at the top to stem the tide and get us back on track. The media did its level best to invoke panic and fear into the hearts and minds of anyone watching or listening.

We saw similar investor reactions during the COVID-19 epidemic, with trading activity significantly increasing as the pandemic unfolded.

Fast forward to today.

Who or what are you listening to? Pundits, who announce that asset allocation is dead and that everyone should sell all their stocks only to follow that with a *mea culpa* just days later?

In a climate where the vast amounts of available financial information are rivaled only by the vast number of economic opinions and the vast numbers of outlets that allow them to chime in, you must figure out what you stand for and where you stand. Separate the noise from the truth and purpose of your planning. With a solid game plan, it doesn't matter whether someone is telling you to buy or sell, especially considering that they have no idea of your particular financial circumstance, needs, or dreams. You accept the news for what it is: temporary financial entertainment and a measuring stick of just how things are doing at that moment. Then, if you're serious about creating, protecting, and passing on your wealth and your values, you tune out the madness, focus on what matters to you and your family, knowing you have planned accordingly.

If you take just one thing from this book, I hope it's the message that you must follow your uniquely crafted plan and not chase the latest headlines or returns. That just doesn't work. A great allegory called "The Smartest Man in the World" illustrates why.

The Smartest Man in the World

There once was a man who was regarded as the Smartest Man in the World. Each year on December 31, he would invest 100 percent of his investable assets into a single asset class, and each year his investment returns were stellar. He always knew the best performing asset class to invest in year after year, according to Callan Associates' Callan Chart. For example, in 2006, he knew to be 100 percent invested in real estate, that year's best-performing asset class. Then in 2008, he knew to switch to 100 percent U.S. Treasuries, that year's best performer. It was an impossible skill, but somehow, he had mastered it.

Each year at a family gathering on New Year's Day, he would tell his family all about his investment success and his brilliant investment clairvoyance. His brother-in-law, who had to endure this bragging about investment performance, decided he would try to replicate the Smartest Man's success by following his investment strategies. However, the brother-in-law was always a year behind the Smartest Man since he did not know what the strategy was until the following New Year, and he assumed if an investment did well last year, it should be okay this year. So, when the Smartest Man was reallocating his portfolio into his next successful pick, the brother-in-law was investing into his old strategy.

For ten years, this went on, and finally, in 2013, the brother-in-law decided to find out why he was not having the same success as the Smartest Man. Below is a summary of his analysis between 2003 and 2012 gross of fees and taxes, which can vary by individual.

INVESTOR	AVERAGE RETURN[1]	STANDARD DEVIATION[2]	RESULTS
Smartest Man	24.3 percent	10.5 percent	The Smartest Man did the impossible; he had high returns and the least volatility as measured by Standard Deviation.
Brother-in-Law	2.7 percent	23.2 percent	By being one year late replicating the Smartest Man's strategy, the brother-in-law ended up with the worst average returns and the highest volatility

Indexing	7.1 percent	18.3 percent	If the brother-in-law would have utilized a passive indexing strategy comprised solely of large cap stocks represented in the S&P 500, he would have performed over 2 ½ times better with over 20 percent less volatility.
Diversified	8.8 percent	12.4 percent	If the brother-in-law would have utilized a diversified strategic investment strategy comprised of 60 percent invested in stocks (25 percent large cap, 20 percent small cap, 15 percent International), 30 percent bonds, and 10 percent REITS, he would have performed 3.2 times better with over 45 percent less volatility.

1. Returns were calculated using the annual return data from 2003-2013 from the following: iShares. Foreign stocks are represented by the MSCI EAFE Index; Large cap stocks are represented by the Standard & Poor's 500® Index; Mid cap stocks are represented by the Standard & Poor's MidCap 400 Index; Small cap stocks are represented by the Standard & Poor's SmallCap 600 Index; Real estate is represented by the Dow Jones U.S. Real Estate Index; US corp bonds are represented by the iBoxx $ Liquid Investment Grade Index; US gov't bonds are represented by the Barclay's U.S. 3–7 Year Treasury Bond Index. This material has been obtained from sources generally considered reliable. No guarantee can be made as to its accuracy. This is not intended to represent or predict the performance of any particular investment. Past performance is not an indicator or guarantee of future results. An investor cannot invest directly in an index.
2. Standard deviation is a commonly used measurement for the amount of risk in an investment. Higher standard deviation signals a more volatile, and therefore risky, investment. Securities offered through ValMark Securities, Inc. Member FINRA, SIPC. 130 Springside Drive, Akron OH 44333-2431 1-800-765-5201

Essentially, you can't time the market perfectly for the same reason that Dad failed so miserably when he was trying to chase those fish. Just as the water temperatures controlled where the swords were, and his late arrival dictated that he would not be able to fish in that sweet spot, current conditions impact a stock's movement and pricing. If you wait to jump until the stock moves up, you'll usually wind up with nothing but leftovers just like Dad did.

As my dad found out the hard way, disregarding all the chatter out there about the best thing to do isn't the easiest thing. So, you need to figure out what *you* stand for and have faith in it.

What Do You Stand For?

So many of the boomers sitting on the laps of their mom or dad (who were born during the Great Depression) were told how safe it was to hold on to your money, bury it in your backyard, or just put it in the bank so that it would always be there. Having had that horrid experience of watching things go so awry, in many cases this older generation foisted their fears onto the next generation along with their assets. So, this inheritance has also come with an emotional attachment to things like stocks, bonds, art, wine, boats, and real estate. Our challenge is to get folks to attach meaning and purpose to those assets—or anything related to money—and visualize that legacy as college tuition for a child, or rental income, or interest from capital that allows you to plan a worthwhile experience for your family and/or friends and toast your benefactor while doing it. That's what helps you stick to—and execute—the game plan instead of indulging in knee-jerk reactions or succumbing to meaningless temptation.

Part of knowing what you stand for involves recognizing that no one is going to get lucky year after year. It doesn't matter how good your advisor or financial planner is. They're not going to swing the bat and hit a home run every time, especially if they're focused on not putting your retirement at risk. Luckily, lots of people have made it to the Hall of Fame with singles and doubles and hitting above average.

The secret lies in creating a game plan that aligns with your values and your philosophy so that no matter what happens, be it death, disability, divorce, recessions, or corrections, you keep sailing.

That's a far cry from chasing the newest stock, fund, or the latest toy. Let's face it. You didn't wake up at age 60, or whenever you decide to retire, with millions in net worth. You knew that nobody needs multiple boats or sports cars. You had a plan. You invested wisely. You recognized that disciplined saving and investing wins out.

Now is not the time to get away from all that disciplined work and all those good habits.

The fact is there will always be something to pursue. People have been chasing tech stocks for years. In the early 2000s, a family that later became a client lost $700,000 chasing tech stocks with a big-name company broker. Thousands of people have taken similar hits, but many keep on looking for that next shiny object that seems like it will yield a huge payout. Next, they'll be chasing marijuana and Bitcoin, thinking they're going to make a lot of money. But what if they don't? What happens if they invest all they have, and the gamble doesn't pay off? This is your future we're talking about.

As I've mentioned in Chapter 4, when I meet with clients who have managed to save millions for retirement, they never say, "Turn it into more millions." They say, "Don't lose it, and let's not take all the risk of the market."

So instead of only looking for high-growth capital appreciation stocks that might be ahead of the curve, like Apple was when it first went public, we invest in many companies and sectors of the market that produce both dividends and products or services we all use every single day. If you are alive and well years from now, chances are we will still be putting diapers on kids' fannies, caffeinating with coffee, driving a car, insuring homes and autos and businesses, turning on a power source, drinking and eating, washing clothes, and brushing our teeth in the morning and again at night. Value investing in the companies that make the consumer staples that citizens around the globe use day after day and week after week may yield lower rewards than growth investing, but it's also thought to have a little less risk. Not everyone needs a big-screen television or an iPhone, but basics—food, clothing, housing, utilities, and cleanliness—will always be a priority.

Investing your money in the companies that make up the fabric of our daily lives may provide more stability, as well as income dividends from the businesses you are familiar with. Or you can go the other route and, feeling sure that you're going to make a killing, you can throw your money at some biotech or pharma company that supposedly has come up with some kind of significant cure. But oops! The pharma breakthrough unexpectedly doesn't get FDA approval, and suddenly you're broke.

Not to mix metaphors, but those golden eggs crack pretty darn easily.

As I've said before, there are many thousands of stocks traded every day. You just can't chase them all. And my advice to you is not to chase them at all. Instead, be clear about what you stand for and honor that.

Bad things happen when you chase, a lesson Dad took to heart. After getting skunked because he was late to the party, he never made that mistake again. He knew that targeting swordfish in known areas at desirable times was a heck of a lot more productive for him.

When he eventually decided to retire from swordfishing, he was resolute and stayed true to that decision as well—a move that saved his life.

"Come with us on one last trip for the season," Billy Tyne, who had replaced Dad as captain of the Andrea Gail, said over the phone. "We're short a man. We need you."

Dad had stopped swordfishing four months prior, in part because it was time to give his body a break, in part because in his words, "That ship had sailed and the swordfishing industry was going downhill and was no longer as lucrative as it once had been," and in part because my mom had wanted him to stop swordfishing for years. So even though his good friend begged him and filled his ears with the potential profits the trip would yield, my dad declined. Besides, he had promised my mom and knew she'd be angry if he went back on his word.

My mom was stern and not a woman to be messed with.

Dad and Mom in their kitchen, where they've created decades of delicious memories.

Dad wouldn't have gone even if Mom had given him her blessing. That white-knuckle trip from Chapter 1 when Hurricane Gabrielle slammed into the Andrea Gail on her way back home still haunted him a year and a half later.

That's not to say he wasn't tempted. But he had decided to trade swordfishing for groundfishing for cod, haddock, and flounder, and had launched himself into the new business. He sure didn't mind the steady paycheck for the family provided by the groundfishing he was doing. Besides, he had committed to another crew.

Knowing what he stood for prevented him from being on the Andrea Gail when it got caught in the perfect storm and sank, killing all aboard.

Sometimes staying the course and hunkering down in port is what guarantees that you'll survive to fish another day.

Miss a Little, Miss a Lot

Once again, the fishing analogy holds with investing. Over the last decade of trading from 7/01/08 through 6/30/18, the S&P 500 was up +10.2 percent per year on a total return basis. If you missed the five best performance days in those ten years, you would have lost out on half the gains you would have otherwise enjoyed. I'm not talking about five days a year. Just missing the five best days of the market over ten years, your average return would have been cut by more than four percentage points to +5.8 percent per year, according to BTN Research.

Of course, an average is just that—an average. Most years don't hit that 10 percent long-term average. Or, like waves rolling in, they're up, down, and all over the place. But that's the point. You need to have your hooks in the water when it's time to fish. Some hooks will come back empty, with not even the bait left. But others will come back with treasure. So, sometimes the right thing to do involves sticking to the plan you committed to and hunkering down instead of doing anything different.

That doesn't mean you do nothing. Think about fishermen. If my dad was gone for 25 days, he fished for less than half of those. The rest of the time was spent on the navigation plan, the prep, following a process, executing the plan, taking care of the catch, and getting home safely, which was the most critical part.

Staying the course financially means that you keep on saving and investing 10–15 percent of your gross earnings during the accumulation phase of life (in good times and bad) since consistent, smaller drips along the way add up to a big overflowing barrel later on. More shares later at higher prices is the goal and a rising tide lifts all boats. So, in good times and bad, you want to be an accumulator of investment shares that you will use for income streams in retirement when that earned income is no longer being harvested.

This is where having a financial captain and a game plan is critical. Otherwise, it's too easy to bail when the skies begin to look threatening or the clouds unleash. If you have a navigation plan that includes disciplined saving and investing, having that financial expertise will also help you ascertain when to retrench or when to set out, confident that you'll return to port safely.

Every once in a while, however, emotions wind up ruling the day. Susan, a long-time client, had given me half a million tax-free dollars of her husband's life insurance policy to manage. We had created a plan for her that included risk mitigation, so when the stock market tanked in 2008, she was fine. But she sure didn't feel fine when that life insurance money took a hit. Even though she had plenty of cash to tap, she called in a panic.

"I can't see this go less than $500,000," Susan said. "We need to get out."

Even though I argued against her request, I understood it. In October 2008, in the eye of the storm, she sold. And she slept better.

She wound up buying back into that same stock portfolio six months later, a move that cost her 1 to 2 percent of her portfolio. Susan recognized that she had made a mistake, but she had needed to bail out for her emotional well-being. The fact that I warned her against it, but ultimately respected her wishes, only deepened the relationship.

It's not always about the money. Most of the time, it's not about the money. It's about everything else. So yes, we will pull the trigger against my better judgment if a client insists. It's their ship after all, and if they're convinced it's time to dock the boat, we'll do that. But believe me, we're going to have a lot of conversations first, especially if their decision is based on sensationalist TV reports.

We know firsthand that retired people are more susceptible to this kind of inflammatory rhetoric because they have a lot more time to immerse themselves in the bad news than do people who are working and/or running after kids. It takes discipline, solid income planning, and ignoring financial reporting that doesn't serve you to stay the course. Because I promise you, there's a line out the door of people waiting for you to turn your paper losses into real ones by selling those shares of stock at a bargain.

On the other hand, since Susan honored two-thirds of the plan we had created, she came out of the Great Recession relatively unscathed. A lot of people can't say the same.

Let me remind you that waiting for things to go south before you seek the counsel of a financial professional is like changing the batteries in your smoke detector after a fire. Wouldn't it be better to think about prevention? Besides, once you and your financial planner have ascertained what you're after and come up with a way to get you there, riding out the storm and sticking with the game plan becomes a lot easier.

Admittedly, having the persistence to invest money when the market is going down, down, down, and the news is all bad is downright difficult. You have to have nerves of steel to continue to invest and buy companies that are off by 40 to 50 percent. But if the plan dictates that you need to save $4 to $5 million to retire and you have to invest $30,000 a quarter or $10,000 a month to achieve that goal, then you take a deep breath, take that $10,000, and buy when everyone else is selling. Sure, that takes a lot of faith, but history tells us that investors are rewarded.

To repeat, you didn't wake up at retirement with millions of dollars by mistake or happenstance. You most likely followed a process or game plan to get this far, and now is not the time to break the great habits that got you here. Instead of thinking about chasing those shiny objects, you need to understand and acknowledge what you and your wealth represent. Attaching meaning to the money gives it great purpose, helps you stick with the plan, and illuminates decisions to be made for you and your future legacy.

Continuing to make the sacrifices needed to save for the future is never easy, that's for sure. Life events, just like the ocean, have a way of humbling us along the way. Whether contending with death, disability, divorce, unemployment, or whatever challenge has been thrown down, you'll never find a straight path to get you where you're headed. But stay the course, and you'll wind up there.

This is totally doable. But you have to commit to a plan, and so many just don't. Many clients seek purpose and clarity with accumulated assets and cannot honestly tell you exactly how much they need or want and for how long they are going to need it. That explains why fewer than 12 percent of U.S. adults have a balance of $1 million or more in their 401k accounts, according to Vanguard. Perhaps most importantly, you have to know what you stand for and not let anything sway you from that.

Life and the financial markets that govern our invested assets have a way of creating rough waves that may throw us off course from time to time. As a financial captain, it's important to continue to monitor, maintain, and maximize planning opportunities.

What we do as financial planners ranges from being watchdogs looking for opportunity to being guard dogs protecting the kitty, otherwise known as your accumulated assets. In good times and in bad, we take care of what's onboard through sound investing strategy. Asset allocation, for example, works to increase potential profit as well as to mitigate risk. It doesn't eliminate it, but it sure makes the ride less bumpy.

One of the biggest lessons from the Great Recession of 2008-2009 is that if your goal or your destination hasn't changed, then selling assets during the craziness and turning paper losses into realized losses is not a good option. Sometimes it's better to ride out the storm instead of trying to get ahead or behind it. With fishing, you may need to pull up the gear, tie-down everything on the boat, and wait to fish another day. Those investors with varied income streams and six to twelve months of expense coverage sitting in cash had a much better and less stressful time riding out the recession of a lifetime.

Don't get me wrong; that doesn't mean our clients—the ones who had been with us for years along with the new ones who hired us when things got ugly—weren't stressed. We all were stressed in those days. I know how much hearing a voice on the other end of the phone helped when things turned ugly. In the eye of the storm, you do not want to be given a 1-800 number. With so much information out there, investors didn't know how many layers of the onion to peel back in 2008 or how any of that related to them. When they got their distribution, they wanted to know that someone was looking out for them. And when they got scared about their plummeting investments, they wanted someone to reassure them or to tell them they needed to take another course of action.

The biggest reason people turned to us in those dark days, however, was that we had a process. Of course, they didn't exactly come in and say, "I need a game plan." They came in shell-shocked because they didn't know what they were doing. That's why we came up with solid financial game plans that included evaluating shortfall needs versus actual income and ensuring they had cash in place as well as income guarantees in their asset mix. In addition, we came up with individualized income and investment plans to create additional meaning and purpose for their assets.

How does all this work?

Let's say that you have $2 million in three accounts. That's great, but if the market plunges 30 percent, what does that really mean to you? How do you know if you have enough? Have you accounted for taxes and inflation? Have you factored in a raise for yourself? What happens if you lose 15 percent but still take out your usual 4 percent?

You need to know those answers. So, we start by figuring out what you need to use your money for and how much you will need. As we saw in Chapter 3, those answers will dictate how you invest. We'll also plan for a category-five storm so you don't need to worry about what's happening during a downturn while you're vacationing in Italy, because the money you can't afford to lose is in a different pot of money where it won't take a loss. All the math tells us that over the last four decades, recessions have lasted 10 to 11 months on average. As a result, we make sure that any of our retired clients who are taking income from assets have a year of cash available to them, so we don't have to sell during a storm when the prices are down.

We followed the above process with each new client. When the markets came back, these new clients realized that we're a little different than most when it comes to our planning process and approach to generating and protecting wealth. We understand that small-percentage mistakes on big chunks of money add up to significant financial pain. Our process is designed to steer you through minor storms as well as big doozies.

When you go looking for a financial planner, remember that this kind of process can get you through the good and the bad. That's what responsible financial planning is all about. Whether it's 30 degrees outside and blowin' a gale wind or 80 degrees, sunny, and calm, hooks need to be baited, then set. That's the only way the fish will put themselves on the hooks while you're sleeping.

This kind of preparation is paramount as you don't want to find yourself needing to create cash flow and being forced to sell in a wild-ride down market when asset prices are falling fast. Nor do you want to have to batten down the hatches, prep the lifeboat, find survival suits, and cut gear loose in the middle of a nasty storm. Smart investing is as much a discipline of avoiding significant loss as it is experiencing great gain.

Investing always entails a certain amount of risk. Risk, by definition, means that we're not in control of the situation. There is, however, one risk that you can control. Instead of falling for everything from media distractions to that sexy new stock, you can make sure you know what you stand for. Your best financial game plan is always the one that works because you persist without distraction, and you're focused on the plan.

There will continually be drama for you to hang your hat on as it relates to reasons why you should or should not invest at any particular moment, including elections, bank defaults, country turmoil, terror attacks, wars, political/geopolitical risks, market risk, interest rates, government shutdowns, debt ceiling issues, disappointing quarterly earnings reports, and financial cliffs. But with your purpose, captain, plan, and process in place, you just need to fish on.

To do that with peace of mind, you must have a financial game plan with meaning that allows you to monitor the financial climate, make adjustments as needed—which we'll talk about in Chapter 7—and get on with the live-, laugh-, and love experience. Staying the course when it comes to the overall plan, however, doesn't mean never deviating by a degree. You will need to adapt to conditions along the way. That's next.

CATCH OF THE DAY:

- Utilize and implement a process to dictate strategy and solutions to maximize your chances for success.
- Have faith in—and stick to—the financial plan you and your financial planner have created, especially during turbulent times. That means blocking out media distractions telling you to act differently. Remember, they're in this for the headlines, clicks, and potentially the institution on the other side of the trade. You're in this for your future.

CHAPTER 6

FISH ON!
THE NEED TO ADAPT

THERE AREN'T MANY FOLKS WHO enjoy surprises. I have found that retirees sure don't. And you can undoubtedly put commercial fishermen in that category. Surprises that happen while fishing on a boat in the middle of the North Atlantic, subject to the whims of Mother Nature and the ocean itself, usually signify something negative. Of course, filling the entire fish hold with swordfish really fast constitutes a nice surprise, but those occurrences are infrequent at best. More often, it's:

- Surprise, the weather and wind patterns are changing for the worse!
- Surprise, we're running low on bait, and the gear is tangled!
- Surprise, we're down to one diesel engine working correctly!

Those are some of the things a swordfish captain thinks about when the word "surprise" is conjured up on a trip. No celebrations with champagne, confetti, and cake come to mind.

Of course, it doesn't matter whether we like surprises or not; life just happens, so surprises will hit. Nothing is perfect, and nothing is permanent. Change is a given.

Life Stages and Life Changes

Although retirement is viewed as a passive period or life stage—one definition of the word retire is "to withdraw to a place of safety"—both your assets and dreams should remain very much in motion and alive. Life can get messy and take unexpected twists and turns. There's a great chance that whatever life hurls at you will impact your financial situation to some degree, so adapting to your situation is essential. According to the Social Readjustment Rating Scale (SRRS), more commonly known as the Holmes and Rahe Stress Scale, six of life's most significant stressors include the death of a spouse (or child), divorce, the death of a close family member, a personal injury or illness, dismissal from work, and retirement.

From this financial practitioner's standpoint, after decades of talking with clients about financial responsibilities, I would add to the stressor mix: marriage, purchasing property, launching a business, funding college tuition, starting a family, and health challenges.

I recently experienced how life-changing an unexpected medical issue can be. Life threw me a curve ball on February 12, 2020, right at the beginning of the global COVID pandemic. I felt worse than I ever have, but chalked it up to a bad case of the flu even though I lost consciousness more times than I care to remember, experienced tachycardia when my heart raced along at more than 200 beats per minute while simply standing from a seated position, and had difficulty walking to my mailbox. The flu symptoms cleared up after a few long days, but the rest did not. It took three-and-a-half months of feeling like a zombie before it was suggested that, like increasing numbers of people with post-COVID long-hauler symptoms, I had post-viral POTS.

"The condition isn't terminal, but it's debilitating. Your life is going to change," the physician told me. He added that I would have to take daily medication for the first time in my life just to help me move about and function.

Two months later I found myself with a POTS cardiologist specialist in Boston who confirmed the diagnosis. I was fighting a circulatory problem. That was the system the COVID virus had attacked. That's why I kept fainting. A temporary drop in blood flow to the brain would hit out of nowhere and I'd pass out and drop to the ground.

I learned that half the POTS sufferers in America are on disability, with the other 50 percent fortunate to feel "normal" again after three to five years of recovery. Determined to fall into the latter category, I threw the kitchen sink at this condition. In addition to my doctor's input and the prescribed medicine to help me retain water and salt, and raise my blood pressure, I sought out another POTS cardiologist (I didn't live near Boston), a physical therapist, and a naturopathic doctor to help with my diet and ridding my body of high toxins because my body was in dysautonomia and couldn't sweat even during my PT three times a week. I also regularly saw a massage therapist for the lymphatic system, an acupuncturist to stimulate the vagus nerve, which controls body functions including heart rate, blood pressure, breathing, and sweating, and a chiropractor to keep me aligned.

Meanwhile, the world had gone to Zoom during the pandemic, and few folks wanted to come into the office, so I would work from home. After 45 minutes to an hour, I'd have to lie down and raise my legs to get the blood back up to my heart and head. Fortunately, although a lot of patients with POTS suffer from pain, I never did.

I was also blessed to be a former athlete and a person of faith—two key elements in my recovery. So, when I felt good enough and the humidity wasn't high, I started walking with my wife at my side. My goal was to eventually reach 6,000 steps a day, but during those first weeks, after just setting out I had to sit down on my neighbor's lawn to rest. Still, I persisted and, eventually, the effort paid off.

The fact that I had three disability policies to cover the mortgage and our monthly living expenses should I not be able to carry out my role as an advisor provided critical peace of mind. It would have been so much harder to focus on my recovery had those not been in place.

"I got this," I would say to myself, knowing I was on track and taking care of business physically, mentally, and financially.

Life passed me by through the window and on a screen during my three-plus years of recovery, but I knew that better, more healthy and productive days lay ahead. In the meantime, I learned a lot about myself, including how to accept help and receive grace. I realized the importance of having a team to support you when you're not at your best. Perhaps most importantly, I recognized that money has limited value if you don't have your health and ability to enjoy it.

Some things happen to us that are out of our control—such is life. Other changes we seek and plan for ourselves. Regardless, the financial impact can be significant unless we've planned ahead. Luckily, having prepared in advance, I didn't have to learn that lesson the hard way. I want to make sure that you don't either.

If you have already retired or are on the verge, dismissal from work is no longer a concern. But the other stressors are relevant financial life events that may cause you to reassess, alter course, and make some potentially serious and impactful money decisions. Even positive life changes—selling a business or a business succession, securing better employment, selling a piece of real estate, receiving an inheritance, the gift of life insurance proceeds, or downsizing real estate assets for a better lifestyle and accessing investable capital for income—require a conversation with your financial planner about what to do next and how to best position the asset with a game plan to accomplish some sort of income, accumulation, or investment goal. Most likely, you will also need to discuss tax considerations, and possibly even estate planning issues.

Life changes don't stop there.

Oh, you've found a new job after your company was sold! Not unusual these days, since many younger employees have five to seven jobs before they're 40 years old. Nonetheless, advancement or change can be good for you professionally and good for your monthly cash flow. Paying down high-interest debt service is necessary and creating an investment account may become a new priority. Remember to rollover your 401k or profit-sharing plan to an IRA if that makes sense, and talk to your investment advisor to figure out how this retirement asset fits into your new financial picture. You may have lost or gained some group benefits in the process of switching jobs or careers as well—make sure your group life and disability insurance policy and medical coverage are still relevant.

Oh, you're starting your own business? Then you probably no longer have an HR Department to go to, so get counsel on how best to approach that challenge of establishing a retirement plan for yourself and others along with a benefits package to attract and retain key people.

Oh, you just had child #3. Congratulations! Time to set up a third 529 education plan and start prepaying college tuition. If one of the children winds up attending private high school, it will be time to pivot again and adapt in order to make that happen. You may also need additional life insurance coverage to cover extra debt service or any loss of spousal income. The amount of life insurance protection really comes down to two factors: you love someone, you owe someone, or a combo of both.

Oh, your child was accepted into their top school or university, and you suddenly realize you haven't saved enough for the $80,000 annual tuition. What are your options?

Or perhaps you realize that downsizing makes more sense than wandering around in an oversize empty nest now that the kids are gone.

Oh, your parents' health is declining, and you're suddenly the primary caregiver and spending two weeks a month taking care of a 90-year-old. Sorry about the new circumstance. Change can come fast to our loved ones as well as ourselves, and often we, too, must adapt. This can be hard emotionally as well as financially since your income is taking a hit now that you're only working part-time. In fact, a 2023 study from CNBC shows that two thirds of those caring for parents are stressed financially.

Clearly, we all have to adapt in all kinds of ways as we go along in our personal and financial lives. We are continually making the necessary changes to limit risk, seize opportunity, and provide ourselves with some sense of calm in the storms of life.

Stop for just a moment, please, and think about what keeps you up at night. What are you worried about deep down? Maybe it's a health condition that could throw you off. Or a divorce. Or the death of someone close to you. Perhaps the prospect of your own demise concerns you. Or maybe you're worried that you're going to outlive your money or lose it all in the next financial crisis.

Most of us instinctively understand how life-changing any of the above circumstances would be for ourselves and/or our loved ones. Things are going to happen; our ability to adapt to the newness of our situation will dictate the eventual outcome. So, we do one of two things:

- We prepare ahead of time—both mentally and financially—to mitigate them as best we can by keeping three to six months' worth of expenses (more if fully retired) as a slush fund for opportunity or crisis protection.
- We push back those thoughts and keep paddling down "da Nile"—aka denial—telling ourselves that these kinds of events can't or won't happen, or that they only happen to other people.

Clearly, the last option is not the smart way to go.

Now that you've gotten the fish on board from the depths of the ocean, we have to consider all the opportunities and issues lurking above and below the waterline that can make or break you. In the process, we look at as many potential scenarios as possible to protect against those unforeseen dangers, starting with one of the biggest concerns for us all—health and well-being. And while we can't do much more to protect ourselves on those fronts other than making healthy choices as we go along, we can protect ourselves on the money front if we think ahead.

So, I have to ask: Do you have a financial game plan should a crisis arise?

For starters, have you set aside enough money, or can you count on guaranteed income sources like an income annuity and Social Security to cover a year or two? Sure, you have plenty of investments, but, as previously noted, it's always wise to have half a year to a full year's worth of income needs in cash equivalents to avoid selling in a declining market. Since you only lose when you sell in a down market, if you don't have to sell when the market takes a nosedive, you won't turn a paper loss into a realized loss.

Second, are there any income guarantees in your assets mix? If you have gone through a planning process and determined what your shortfall is on need vs. actual income, then it may be wise to fund that delta with an income annuity strategy that you cannot outlive. (You might want to take another look at Chapter 4 for a refresher about how to do that.)

When these two things are done in tandem, anxiety over spending too much or selling at an inopportune time becomes muted. The assets at risk can ride out the storm, and you can continue to eat, drink, sleep well, and thrive in retirement, even knowing that life's inevitable changes are just around the corner.

Live Well and Prosper

Luckily, the kinds of crises we've been discussing aren't the norm. So, while you do need to prepare for them, don't forget that you're not just planning for emergencies. You're also planning for the rest of what will hopefully be a very long, happy life.

To be prepared when it comes to finances, you have to assess your current position in terms of cash flow, expenses, savings, and budgeting. Are you on target to meet your retirement goals? If not, how much more do you need to save and how does that money need to be invested so that you'll reach those goals while limiting your risk exposure? If you have kids and still need to think about college, the same kind of analysis is required. And since the only guarantees in life are death and taxes, you need to make sure that you and your family are protected on those fronts as well. So, you also must consider long-term healthcare, disability insurance, and life insurance, all of which we'll address in Chapter 7.

In short, you have to focus on how retirement is going to impact your finances and evaluate your progress as you go. Remember, the earned-income train comes to a full stop when you retire, a fact that can be a game-changer. Income and assets lost are much more difficult to earn back when you're no longer earning. Whether you're on track, off track, way off course, way ahead, or way behind, you have to know your exact position to deal with life's surprises. My dad couldn't be near the fish; he had to be on the fish.

Similarly, mistakes are much more costly once you move from the accumulation phase to the distribution stage of your financial life. Losing 20 percent without adding additional funds to your IRA or 401k because you've retired requires a 25 percent gain just to get back to even. This problem is compounded too when you're taking distributions from a declining asset base.

The best way to protect yourself against devastating financial mistakes is to regularly review your ever-changing situation and your finances with your financial planner. In this chapter, we'll talk a lot more about what needs to drive those changes. For now, all you have to remember is that your conversation shouldn't be about whether the market is up or down, but rather about where you're at in terms of your financial plan. When I meet with clients who are just moving into retirement, I can't say things are going to be okay if I don't know where we're supposed to be relative to investments and withdrawals. Only by reviewing what they have, how they're investing their resources, and how much they're taking out each month can we determine where they're headed. And that's rarely a straight line, although it can appear that way on a sheet of paper.

My dad taught me that there are no straight lines—literally and figuratively—when swordfishing. He knew he was going to the Grand Banks because that was where the fish were. But ocean navigation is not linear, because the world is not flat. As you already know, when you leave Gloucester, you can't just head north. Instead, because of the curvature of the earth, you have to head due east and get into the Gulf Stream before heading north to the fishing grounds. You also have to account for the fact that a nautical mile equals 1.15 land miles due to all those wave-related ups and downs between the port you left and your destination. In addition, if you want to get there and catch fish, you have to assess the winds, the current, and the basic navigation plan as you go. Maintaining a course and altering your course are both necessary.

No Straight Lines in Life

Just as there are no straight lines on the sea, there are no straight lines in life either. When you're ready to set your cruise control, life has a funny way of forcing you to address changes that happen as you enter a new life stage or changes that just pop up.

I'm a great example of there being no straight lines in life. I entered the financial service business in 1997 with a captive insurance agency that had a great, strong story behind it, along with about a hundred-year history. The financial offerings were solid, and the training program for a novice like me was necessary and productive. There were several such agencies in the Boston area, but I had a local connection to this particular agency, and I wanted to start my career where I knew some folks. It's hard enough building a business from scratch, and at the time, financial reps who were starting out experienced an 80 percent fail rate within their first 24 months.

I wanted to be in the other 20 percent.

Correction. I *had* to be in the other 20 percent.

I had left a teaching-coaching position with a steady income and benefits, including a retirement pension waiting for me decades later if I stayed. But I couldn't hang around as I had a long-held vision and personal dream to pursue. I also had the sense to know that if I was ever going to make the leap, it would have to be before we started a family and had a big mortgage. My supportive, young wife understood this, and she encouraged me to jump ship and pursue another course. She had known me as someone who had always wanted to be in the financial service business to help people with money issues. In fact, unlike my fish captain dad, who ended up skippering a swordboat even though he had never dreamed of doing that, I had envisioned being a businessman since the eighth grade. Dad was all for it.

Yup, I had a plan, one my father had endorsed. Yet despite entering college with economics as my declared major, I wound up with a degree in Spanish and a certification to teach. No straight lines! After teaching for three years, I realized it was time to reclaim the original dream.

So, I took a calculated risk, not unlike the one Dad had made in 1980 when he signed on to his first swordfishing trip as a deckmate in the hopes of creating a better financial situation for the family. And it worked. I became a successful advisor within a large corporate structure. Although I didn't have a single client and definitely no guaranteed paycheck, I had a plan along with plenty of energy and naïveté. So, I set out to knock on the doors of 100 people I knew well and build a business. Luckily my plan succeeded.

After six years, my achievements—to say nothing of the perks that included a corporate-sponsored benefit plan (medical, dental, retirement, expense allowance)—were downright reassuring. Even so, my business partner David S. McKechnie, CLU®, CAP® and I realized that we didn't like the limitations of the broker-dealer that existed at the time on the investment side of our business. Our investment advisory business was growing by leaps and bounds, and we wanted to be able to offer our clientele opportunities for growth in stock, bond, mutual fund, and ETF offerings not available through the company we worked for. So, having established Beauport Financial Services as a name and entity three years before, we traded in our comfort zone and went the independent route.

Our mission statement sums up not only what makes us different from other financial advisors, but why we walked away from a sure thing to form our own wealth management company:

Our dedicated focus is a custom, caring partnership** that's unique for each client. It's a client-centered relationship built for success, providing purpose, clarity, and peace of mind in an established planning process designed to assist clients in attaining their goals.* ***We craft custom financial solutions *to assist each client's unique aspirations.*

What we've been able to achieve for our clients—and the satisfaction we take from that—has justified all the discomfort we had to endure while adapting to our new reality.

Adaptability

I probably learned how best to adapt from watching my dad and listening to his stories. Even now, he surprises me.

"What was something unexpected or weird that you found on the end of your hook while swordfishing?" I recently asked him.

"There was this thin, 11-foot, serpentine fish, almost fluorescent in color, with fangs and a head shaped like a seahorse," he answered. "We called it the Devilfish and tossed it back. I still have no idea what it was."

He sure recognized the other surprise—a massive great white shark. When they brought it alongside the port side of the boat, it seemed lifeless and limp. Captain Charlie wanted the shark's teeth. So, he lay down on his stomach and had the crew hold his lower legs and ankles as he hung over the opened gate at the side of the boat so he could cut off the shark's head. The moment the chainsaw bit into the shark's flesh, it lurched up and sideways, scaring the life out of Dad. Fortunately, the crew yanked him back in the boat, allowing him to escape the bite of those teeth he coveted. Talk about rapidly adapting to changing circumstances!

It takes a strong team to make it all happen at home and at sea.

Thankfully, preparation, adaptation, and responsiveness (Dad's along with his crew's) kept Dad alive and made his successes and our celebrations more frequent than the inevitable disappointments due to lack of fish or disappointingly low prices.

Dad's adaptation wasn't reserved for the Andrea Gail. Since swordfishing is so seasonal, he learned to fish for different species on different vessels during different seasons. But that didn't mean he didn't have to contend with a lot of scary crap along the way. Eventually, he figured he had gambled on his safety enough, and it was time to adapt to unchangeable things like growing older, to say nothing of finally acceding to my mom's steadfast insistence that he stop swordfishing.

Even after he switched to full-time groundfishing, he continued to adapt. He had to since every new fishing season meant a different targeted species. Being attuned to those nuances led to some banner trips.

"I got a feeling," he recalled about one late fall trip when he was groundfishing on the 90-foot Corey Pride.

At the time, grey sole was fetching a nice price at the dock, so he decided to go after that. On a hunch and despite a forecast for foul weather, he headed to a fertile area called the Pistol near Jeffreys Ledge, which he had learned about from other captains, and threw out his nets. In 24 hours and three tows, he harvested 13,000 pounds of grey sole from the flat, sandy bottom and made it back 24 hours ahead of the storm. Bam! Each crew member collected $1,500 bucks, with Dad earning an extra half share since he was the captain. His calculated risk had paid off. Yes, a storm was on its way, but he knew he could trust his instruments and the big lumbering sturdy boat that had just had some work done on it. And he knew he could turn around if it got too hairy since he was just hours (instead of days) away from home.

The crew, of course, was delighted. So was the Corey Pride's owner.

"It beat going to the bar and drinking that previous night," Dad told me, especially since when they returned to that same spot two days later, after the storm had passed, they wound up getting shut out.

Sometimes prayers are answered—in part because Dad did all he could to put the odds on his side while still doing what was needed to come home with the goods. He used his instruments and gathered data to avoid unnecessary risk, always evaluating the risks he ran in terms of the potential reward. He made a point of continually assessing and taking inventory of what was required for the current trip. He also took stock of future needs, which we'll talk about in the next chapter.

Unfortunately, even the most meticulous preparation doesn't always work. Memories of broker trips still hurt—when the only thing he had to show for a month at sea was a weathered boat, crew members that were as tired as they were miserable, and even more calloused hands and gray hairs. Dad recalled dressing out 6,000 pounds of fish, which took many man-hours of physical labor, not to mention the cost of fuel, equipment, and gear required to get the fish on the boat, only to get a low price per pound at the fish auction on the dock. Of course, he also had to contend with a disappointed boat owner holding a fist full of bills and invoices for thousands of dollars from the diesel company, the grocery store, the boatyard, the mechanic, the supply store, and the insurance company. Years later, he remains frustrated about losing money on those trips. Physical labor is always a difficult way to earn a living, and when you're punished for your efforts rather than being rewarded, it stings.

Still, he knew that was just part of the business, and if he let his experience and expertise dictate, he would put the odds in his favor. Only once did he take a huge risk without knowing the lay of the land, and that broker trip haunts him way more than the others.

Only a few days were left in the swordfishing season that fall. The Andrea Gail had already been at sea for a month. It was going to be impossible to get home to unload the fish and squeeze in another trip to the Grand Banks. Suddenly, the boat owner came up with a plan. Instead of going all the way back to Gloucester, why not have a freezer truck meet the boat in Nova Scotia? While the truck transported the catch to Boston, where it could be sold, Dad could quickly refuel and restock necessities and head back out to Grand Banks, saving about a week.

Since time was of the essence in the waning days of the short North Atlantic fall swordfishing season, Dad agreed to this new strategy. So, he pulled into Louisburg, Nova Scotia, unloaded $104,000 worth of swordfish onto the truck, and headed back out. On the way home, after catching another $45,000 of new swordfish, he learned that the shipping truck had been held up at the Canadian-U.S. border because it wasn't properly registered or bonded. Then it was determined that the catch had to be taken to Philadelphia to be inspected by the FDA for mercury content before being sold. Okay, not great, but the fish was still frozen, right?

Not exactly.

The truck wound up sitting in the FDA facility with its freezer units off, so the fish started to rot. Eventually, it was sent to Hyannis, MA, where it sold for cents (rather than dollars) on the pound to be used as cat food.

Dad was as livid and disgusted as his crew. Despite all the work that had been done correctly, he wound up netting a measly $1,000 for the entire trip. He'd been away from his family for 43 days—a full one-fifth of his seven-month fishing season— with next to nothing but frustration to show for it. He never again let the swordfishing season dictate the strategy or convince him to deviate from the plan he knew worked.

Yes, even the best plans sometimes get skewed. Sometimes you do everything right, but things still don't work out, and you don't make any money. You may know where your sweet spot is, but as we've seen, the trip there won't be linear, and it surely isn't guaranteed. That's when you have to adapt. (There's that word again!)

Note that I did not say that you have to abandon ship.

Keep Sailing, Keep Fishing

It has been said that the pain of losing 10 percent on your portfolio far outweighs the joy of earning 10 percent. Still, it's not wise to become overly conservative with the assets that need to carry you decades into your retirement journey. Your money must continue to work for you. This is not the time to drop anchor in port and refuse to move. You've set sail, and you need to keep sailing. Your income plan and financial planning timeline will dictate what specific action you must take and when. And when those storms arise, as they will, just remember that the financial markets are efficient and have worked consistently over the long haul.

Take a look at the Historical Achievement Rates chart below, and you'll find return rates that have been averaged from 1926 to 2016. With the moderately-aggressive portfolio, which as opposed to the second stock-only portfolio, consists of 75 percent stocks, and 25 percent bonds and cash, you'll achieve a 6 percent rate of return 100 percent of the time over a 20-year period. If you've got 30 years during which to leave that investment untouched, on average, you'll achieve an 8 percent return 100 percent of the time.

Remember, this chart averages return rates over the last 90 years, including the Great Depression, which was not exactly a banner time for investing.

All this is great if you've planned for your retirement well in advance. But even if you haven't, you've still got plenty of fishing ahead of you. Let's say you retire in your mid-60s, and you plan on being alive at 85. That means you've got a 20-year runway in front of you. You could knee-jerk and move all your investments to bonds and cash to protect them, but why would you not choose to own stocks if historically a properly managed portfolio over 20 years has a 100 percent chance of delivering 6 percent returns and a 98.61 percent chance of delivering 7 percent. I'd take that bet every day and twice on Sunday.

MODERATELY AGGRESSIVE PORTFOLIO (HISTORICAL ACHIEVEMENT RATES)
FIXED INCOME 25% | LARGE CAP EQUITY 20% | MONEY MARKET 0% | AGGRESSIVE EQUITY 55%

	0%	4%	6%	7%	8%	9%	10%	12%
5 YEAR	91.95%	83.91%	80.46%	77.01%	74.71%	66.67%	63.22%	48.28%
10 YEAR	100.00%	96.34%	87.80%	86.59%	82.93%	75.61%	70.73%	48.78%
20 YEAR	100.00%	100.00%	100.00%	98.61%	97.22%	94.44%	81.94%	50.00%
30 YEAR	100.00%	100.00%	100.00%	100.00%	100.00%	96.77%	91.94%	58.06%

AGGRESSIVE PORTFOLIO (HISTORICAL ACHIEVEMENT RATES)
FIXED INCOME 0% | LARGE CAP EQUITY 15% | MONEY MARKET 0% | AGGRESSIVE EQUITY 85%

	0%	4%	6%	7%	8%	9%	10%	12%
5 YEAR	89.66%	81.61%	79.31%	77.01%	75.86%	71.26%	66.67%	52.87%
10 YEAR	97.56%	93.90%	86.59%	82.93%	80.49%	76.83%	74.39%	60.98%
20 YEAR	100.00%	100.00%	98.61%	98.61%	97.22%	94.44%	86.11%	69.44%
30 YEAR	100.00%	100.00%	100.00%	100.00%	100.00%	100.00%	96.77%	79.03%

The examples given are hypothetical, for illustrative purposes only and does not reference any specific client experience. Performance of an index is not illustrative of any specific investment. Indices are not managed and do not incur fees or expenses. It is not possible to invest directly in an index. Data source: Ibbotson & associates: 1926 – 1994; Bloomberg 1996-2016 Money Market – Data Source: 1926-1994 IA SBBI U.S. 30-Day Treasury Bill Index is an unweighted index that measures the performance of 30-day maturity U.S. Treasury bills. Data Source 1994-2016: The BofA Merrill Lynch US 3-Month Treasury Bill Index is comprised of a single issue purchased at the beginning of the month and held for a full month. At the end of the month that issue is sold and rolled into a newly selected issue. Large Cap Equity – Data Source 1926-1994 Ibbotson Associates SBBI S7P 500 TR – Tracks the performance of domestic S&P 500 index stocks. Data Source 1994-2016 Bloomberg SPTX Standard and Poor's 500 Index is a capitalization-weighted index of 500 stocks. The index is designed to measure performance of the broad domestic economy through changes in the aggregate market value of 500 stocks representing all major industries. Aggressive Equity – Data Source 1926-1994 The IA SBBI U.S. Small Cap Stock Index is a custom index designed to measure the performance of small capitalization U.S. stocks. Data Source 1994-2016 The S&P SmallCap 600® measures the small-cap segment of the U.S. equity market. Fixed Income – Data Source 1926-1994 U.S. Long Term (15+ year) Corporate Bond Index Ibbotson Associates SBBI US LT Corp – An index that tracks high grade long term corporate bonds. U.S. Long Term US Treasury Index IA SBBI US LT Govt TR: The total returns from 1977-present are constructed with data from The Wall Street Journal. The data from 1926-1976 are obtained from the Government Bond File at the Center for Research in Security Prices (CRSP) at the University of Chicago Graduate School of Business. To the greatest extent possible, a one bond portfolio with a term of approximately 20 years and a reasonably current coupon-whose returns did not reflect potential tax benefits, impaired negotiability, or special redemption or call privileges-was used each year. Where "flower" bonds (tenderable to the Treasury at par in payment of estate taxes) had to be used, the term of the bond was assumed to be a simple average of the maturity and the first call dates minus the current date. The bond was "held" for the calendar year and returns were computed. Domestic High Yield Corporate Bond Index BarCap U.S. Corporate High-Yield Index - Covers the USD-denominated, non-investment grade, fixed-rate, taxable corporate bond market. The index excludes Emerging Markets debt. The Index was created in 1986, with index history backfilled to January 1, 1983. The U.S. Corporate High-Yield Index is part of the U.S. Universal and Global High-Yield Indices. Data source 1994-2016 - U.S. - Long Term (15+ year) Corporate Bond Index The BofA Merrill Lynch 15+ Year US Corporate Index is a subset of The BofA Merrill Lynch US Corporate Index (an index which tracks the performance of US dollar denominated investment grade corporate debt publicly issued in the US domestic market) including all securities with a remaining term to final maturity greater than or equal to 15 years. U.S. Long Term US Treasury Index The BofA Merrill Lynch 15+ Year US Treasury Index is a subset of The BofA Merrill Lynch US Treasury Index (an index which tracks the performance of US dollar denominated sovereign debt publicly issued by the US government in its domestic market) including all securities with a remaining term to final maturity greater than or equal to 15 years. Domestic High Yield Corporate Bond Index The BofA Merrill Lynch US High Yield Index tracks the performance of US dollar denominated below investment grade corporate debt publicly issued in the US domestic market.

When I share the above chart with my clients, I say, "Hey, I know you're 60, and I know you want to put your money in something safe and conservative, but we have to have the conversation about owning some stocks for the long term. Because if you want to earn 7 percent on your money and only 55 percent of it is invested in stocks, then you'd better have a 30-year time horizon for that other 45 percent in fixed income because based on the last 90 years on average, that's how long you'll have to wait to earn that 7 percent."

Of course, these are just averages, so it's important to stay diversified. But it's also critical to remember that you've got to hang in there and keep fishing, even when you feel like jumping ship. History tells us that the stock market always comes around, and always delivers if you're smart about how you invest and have enough time ahead of you to let the market produce.

Assessing the Trip As You Go
Okay, you're convinced that you'll be better off staying with the vessel (i.e., investing) than leaping over the side. Now what?

In Chapters 3 and 5, we talked about the importance of sticking to an investment plan for it to work. But that doesn't mean that you don't change it along the way if it's not working as well as it might.

Dad would always assess his trips, good or bad. Whether contending with stormy seas or lake-like calm, when he headed home after doing the tough stuff, he would evaluate what could have worked more efficiently. Had he caught more tuna than swordfish, or worse yet, too many sharks? Had he allowed the current to push them too far to the east before getting the boat back into line again? Would trying a new spot make sense? Had he stocked up on enough diesel fuel to comfortably make it back to port?

His overall assessment of what worked, what didn't and why, and what could have functioned better included taking the measure of the vessel, the gear, the engine, and the supplies. If any equipment needed fixing, he got on that right away. He and the crew had to make good use of downtime on the way home and be well prepared before the boat ever hit the dock since any needed repairs had to be scheduled ahead of time, and the appropriately skilled mechanic or boat repairman called to Rose's Wharf to do the work. In addition, he needed to determine how much food would be required on the next trip so it could be ordered, along with any needed supplies and gear, while still at sea, and promptly picked up and stored once they off-loaded the fish at the dock.

Minimizing the turnaround time at home was essential if they were going to have a profitable season. Ideally, they would be in port for just four days, but certainly no longer than seven. He even looked at the lunar calendar to ascertain when he would need to catch the quarter moon and head back out, which by the time he reached his destination, would allow him to fish on the full moon for most of the nightly setouts.

He also took measure of the crew's morale and did what he could to make them feel positive. That included making sure they got as much rest as possible by being as efficient as possible. Instead of having all the crew on deck at the same time, he would ask those working to do a little more so the others (and themselves, later) could get some downtime.

This no-drama, cool-cat captain always prepped for tough times and conditions at sea, but also recognized that maintaining a good vibe and work atmosphere on board usually led to a fruitful trip and healthy paycheck back at the dock. He wanted his guys to be happy and feel respected for the labor they were performing. If he managed that correctly, chances were they would return for another trip, and he could keep the crew intact and not have to train another greenhorn or find one on the dock or over a beer in the bar room. Dad may have been in the fishing business, but he was also in the people business and needed to contend with his crew's emotions. Similarly, I may be in the money business, but I'm also in the business of working with the emotions that people attach to their assets.

Dad mastered his trade by initially observing other captains, by doing the work himself, and ultimately by managing the whole process and relying upon the input of his crew along with a master list that started with the engineer and the engine room since a boat can't fish without the dual diesel engines working at full potential. During the five- to six-day steam home (basically a week or two before the next trip), Dad would walk through the engine room with Marvin and review fuel filters, fuel, lubricant, grease, hydraulic oil, nuts and bolts and fittings, light bulbs, tools, welding materials, generators, batteries, etc., making notes on a pad regarding what was needed and what wasn't.

Next, the senior crewman would walk Dad through the inventory he'd done in the gear room, including fishing supplies, beacons and an antenna, knives for gutting the fish, and saw blades to cut the head and sword off.

Then the cook in the galley would check stock on shelves, freezer, and fridge, and plan the meals for the next trip so he could present Dad with a grocery list. Dad would finish the list in the pilothouse and take inventory on any technology upgrades and equipment fixes that needed addressing or parts needing to be replaced.

They all realized that they had to make time to prep and prioritize the next trip. It's easy to recognize the need for all hands to respond in a crisis, as it could mean life or death. It's more difficult to take the time to assess and evaluate when all is well and no issues are occurring, but that's exactly what ensures survival.

Assessment and adaptation are just as critical when it comes to retirement planning. The plan has to morph as conditions change and as you age. As my story and my dad's story show, things shift as you go, so altering course on both your life and your financial front is often necessary. In short, you need to be adaptable, if for no other reason than your needs transform as you enter new life stages. You might wind up becoming more income-focused when you're in your 60s and 70s because you need to be if you're no longer bringing home a paycheck.

On the other hand, if you've accumulated enough over the years, your agenda will probably be to keep those funds relatively safe so that they last the rest of your life. As a result, you may not want to own these go-go growth-type stocks anymore because you don't need them. Either way, you have to have those conversations, and your portfolio has to adapt.

Your decision to change or stay the course will be based upon current and predicted future conditions. Are you going to experience setbacks during the imperfect storm of retirement? Absolutely. Things will go awry at some point, no matter how perfect the plan or how ideal the conditions. Regrettably, you can expect occasional chaos in both your life and your finances, especially since the world is always in some state of flux at best and in some state of bedlam at worst.

While careful planning can mitigate certain situations, as we've seen, some things are always out of your control. For my father, those included the weather, the cost of 20,000 gallons of diesel fuel, and the price per pound he received for the fish he had worked so hard to haul on board. For investors, those out-of-control elements include the stock market and anything that impacts the stock market. So, you want to minimize the external factors, stay positive and focused on the internal factors, and check to see how you're doing when it comes to your financial end goal. As I've noted before, you need to check whether you're on track, off track, way off course, way ahead, or way behind.

Sure, you'll have peaks and troughs, just like Dad did. However, if you know your destination as well as how and when you'll get there, these lows or highs don't become epic events. They're just obstacles to navigate around.

Luckily, numbers know no emotion and always tell the truth. Again, this is where your financial advisor and those regular financial checkups come in. You don't buy a Maserati and never change the oil or never bring it in for inspection unless you want to wind up with a broken-down car. To keep it running, you have to maintain it along the way and take it to the shop periodically, just as you have to keep a close eye on your retirement plan and adjust it as needed.

Yes, just like everything else, your financial plan has to be maintained. And that gets us back to diving in and assessing how things are going—and back to that Maserati. You can't evaluate the engine of your car if you're not lifting open the hood, changing spark plugs, getting in there, and getting dirty.

So, you need to lift up the hood on your financial state of affairs and have those conversations about where you stand since like Dad, you're going to keep going back out and taking those risks. During those financial check-ups and check-ins, you want to talk about what's going on. What's changed? Are you spending more? Do you require less? How are your assets doing? Is it time to rebalance the portfolio, or take some profit off the table, sell, and reposition?

And perhaps the biggest question of all: How do you know that you're on track?

To answer some of these questions and ascertain whether you're on target with your retirement goals, you need to keep score and identify checkpoints along the way. We call that achieving retirement clarity (ARC™) and use the ARC™ Blueprint to assess your progress, make necessary changes, and alter course if needed. One of the first things to consider is how much risk you're taking to generate the return you're getting. If a five percent rate of return is going to ensure that you have plenty of money—with some leftover—even if you live to age 96, why tempt the fates with potentially higher yield but riskier investments?

These financial reviews are vital since staying on course on this journey is paramount. I'll say it again. Every degree counts on the navigation plan if a successful destination is to be enjoyed, since one degree off course early on leads to many nautical miles of difference from your waypoint later on. In short, you always need to check where you're at versus where you're headed.

Keeping Score and Getting Clear

On a swordfishing boat, the captain is always monitoring even before the boat leaves the dock, looking at weather patterns, tide charts, the lunar calendar, talking to other fishermen about where they may be heading and when, assessing the boat as well as the diesel engine, the equipment, the supplies, and even the crew members. It's all part of the big picture. It doesn't matter how great and sturdy the boat is—or even how great the captain is—should a key piece of equipment malfunction. If the ice machine breaks when you're out at sea and can't be repaired, you might as well just turn around and go home because the fish is going to rot no matter how well everything else is going.

Similarly, a solid financial planner assesses your financial state of affairs, making sure that at age 45, 50, 55, and beyond, you're saving what you need while protecting your income, even as you account for changes in health, income needs, and the general economic environment.

The resulting cash flow analysis and timeline for using those assets also help you know what you can and can't afford to do right now. Need a new roof? That's great. You're on target. Or maybe you're $20,000 ahead of goal even though there's been some stormy weather outside.

Of course, that regular assessment—the constant processing of information and data presented right in front of you—only helps if it's accompanied by a willingness on your part to make the best possible decision regarding your survival and prosperity. That means that if you're behind on that retirement goal, you may have to delay getting that new roof until you make up some ground as you continue to fish.

In short, you have to not only ensure that everything is in tip-top shape when you leave the dock, but that it continues to work the way it needs to after you've set sail. To do that, you check in regularly. If you're having a great trip while swordfishing, you ask why. The answer will be that the bait is sitting in 68-degree water in the Gulf, and that's where the fish are. If you're having a crummy trip, you ask why. Maybe the answer is that you've been spending 50 percent of your time untangling the nets and looking for the radio beacon, and so you know what's got to change on the next set. Or maybe the answer is that your expenses and the amount of money you're spending to maintain the vessel are eating into your profits.

Too many investors just look at the returns to make decisions, rather than also considering the cost of ownership and the components of their investments. If two swordfishing boats catch the same amount of fish, the captain who has controlled the outgo is going to be a lot better off than the other one even if they get the same amount of money per pound. In short, to do well, a fishing captain has to focus not only on filling the hold but also on his expenditures and the price he can get for the catch.

You need to assess your financial plan in the same way. As we discussed in the last chapter, this evaluation isn't about whether you're following the plan that's been set forth to a tee, because no one does. You can try your best to do that, but as we've seen, things change. That's why every trip—and every investor—needs a good captain who knows not only how to chart the course, but also when to change course and alter the plan. Your mission when you talk with your advisor at each review is to discuss the macro and microeconomic landscape regarding how things are going, so together you can decide whether anything substantial needs to change or be addressed. And one of the biggies you'll want to examine is whether you're getting the appropriate tax breaks.

To Recap
In this chapter and the previous one, we talked about expecting and preparing for change, but not letting current temporary conditions permanently alter the course of your entire journey. Sure, you'll want to hedge your bet and come up with a strategy that manages risk when rough financial seas call for that. You and your financial planner can discuss how to adjust your investments accordingly. You may even want to explore transferring your risk to a third party, in this case, an insurance company. While that caps your upside, it also protects you from losing money. What you don't want to do is fall into the risk-avoidance trap, no matter how tempting, since inflation alone will guarantee that you'll lose money if you pull all your investments out of the market.

I know it's distressing to experience the market's swings, but you have to stay in the game and execute the plan if you don't want to turn paper losses into real ones. You have to keep fishing. The little chart below from Ben Carlson, author of *The Wealth of Common Sense*, says it all. You'll be fine if you give yourself 10 to 20 years, invest properly for your situation while addressing any identified risks (more on this in the next chapter), and perform a financial check-up with a trusted advisor at least annually.

60/40 Portfolio: 1926-2018

Time Frame	Positive	Negative
Quarterly	70%	30%
One Year	80%	20%
5 Years	95%	5%
10 Years	100%	0%
20 Years	100%	0%

60% S&P 500 / 40% 5 Year Treasuries

Of course, as you can also see from the chart, as your time frame shrinks, the volatility escalates right along with your chance of losing money. That's an important note. You can't judge or expect shorter-term results to predict longer-term success. Neither the numbers nor history lie!

It's not always easy to hang tight when things look grim. Just as fishing requires physical and mental strength, especially when conditions turn challenging, investing has so much to do with behavior and staying the course when the news is awful and gloomy with no rainbow in sight. Even then, there's no need to scrap the entire financial plan because of a bad month or year in the stock market. Your course will certainly have to be altered, and you will need to know what to expect. But adapting doesn't necessarily mean trading in and out of investment positions every quarter and investing in something different altogether. Adapting does mean that you must monitor events closely and pay close attention to the economic environment as a whole and react appropriately.

Once you figure out what's working and what's not, and whether it's time to stay the course or change direction, you can evaluate together what specific changes to enact right away and what can wait. While you're at it, don't neglect those "what-if" discussions. Have you addressed any dangers that might be lurking in your financial plan or portfolio head-on and played out those 'what if' scenarios?

We'll talk more about protecting yourself from potential risks in the next chapter. For now, however, it's time to figure out where you stand on that front. What part of your financial plan is designed to weather a significant storm or survive a correction or recession? Have you set aside six months to a year of living expenses, so you aren't forced to sell assets in a chaotic down market? Have you followed a planning process that will mitigate investment risk in your income planning design? When another recession occurs, and it will, how do you plan to address how that affects your assets? Best to plan when the skies are sunny, and the seas are calm, with a clear mind and no anxiety, so that you have options when things get rough.

Life Stages and Related Financial Considerations
Here's another way to think about the steps to consider during the pre-retirement phases of your life.

- What do getting married, buying a first home, starting a family, or starting a business have in common? They all may trigger your first purchase of life insurance coverage. There are two reasons for buying life insurance: you love someone, you owe money on something, or a combination of the two. Life insurance can pay off any debt owed and/or replace income needed to fund

dreams, tuitions, and life celebrations like a marriage. Or it can simply give someone a hand up when you're not around.
- Once the kids arrive, it's wise to think about funding a 529 plan for future college costs. If, after starting a family, you decide to have one income-earner and one stay-at-home parent, it's paramount that the income-earner own some form of group or private disability insurance to replace the lost income in the event of a prolonged disability event. Bills don't stop even if the income does.
- If you switch jobs, change careers, secure a better opportunity, or cash-in stock options from your company, you may want to rollover your 401k plan to an IRA. For tax-free income when you retire, consider making that a Roth IRA. Starting a Roth IRA early in life can be an excellent plan no matter what's happening on the work front.
- Do you have excess cash flow? Nice! Want to start an investment account to seek better yields and total returns rather than leaving most everything in your bank account? Set up a liquid investment account to beat the bank rate and begin to accumulate wealth outside of your 401k or IRA.
- Should a family member pass and leave you an inheritance, the need for an investment strategy becomes apparent—time to set up a brokerage account for asset growth or income desires. On the other hand, you might not want to wait that long.

Here's how the above looks like in my life. Karen and I got married at 24, bought life insurance at 25, purchased our first home at 26 along with more life insurance, started having kids at 29, which meant more life coverage as well as 529s.

On the job front, I changed careers at 25 (rolling over my IRA on the way out the door). When we became a single-income family in our early 30s, we purchased a disability plan for me. Self-employment meant religiously funding my retirement account and budgeting accordingly. Once all the kids were in school, Karen went back to work, thereby allowing us to start an investment brokerage account with the extra cash flow.

Many of life's events and seasons require some appropriate financial thought and response. When there are important decisions to be made, it's nice to get proper advice and not feel alone. As I've pointed out a number of times, it's essential to have a financial plan as well as a captain in the wheelhouse to guide your financial ship appropriately and see everything through with you. That's even more true when the storms of life happen.

CATCH OF THE DAY:

- In the introduction, I asked you if you had enough to retire on reliably and how you knew that it would provide a lifetime of income. You now understand why it's crucial to have a plan for all seasons—a sturdy ship with a great crew, reliable equipment, a skilled captain who cares deeply, and a navigation plan. But that plan has to be monitored and has to be adaptable to both market and life conditions.
- Your investment journey will be rough at times, but you will get to port, assuming you take stock along the way.

CHAPTER 7

STEAMING BACK HOME & TAKING STOCK

Most of us would love just to have to do things once. Imagine if our children—whether young or grown—got the message (about anything) the first time around. Or if our cars only needed to be serviced when we bought them. Or, for that matter, if a single check-up with the doctor guaranteed good health forever. Life, of course, doesn't work that way. Neither does your financial game plan. So, when it comes to your asset allocation plan, which should be outlined in your investment policy statement (IPS), don't expect to set it, then forget it.

As we've seen, having a plan means that you are modifying it as you go along. What you do at 65 or early on in the retirement journey in terms of your investments is probably not going to be the same as what you do when you're 75 and then 85. Life will have changed. Your income needs and goals may have changed. Those will impact not just how much money you'll need to access, but how that money should be positioned strategically. If, at some point, you wind up needing a bunch more income for three to five years, for example, and your investments are in a capital appreciation portfolio, changes will have to be made. As a result, you have to make sure you're in good hands when it comes to your planner and the plan.

I grew up learning about change and protecting the harvest because when it came to swordfishing, my dad was the planner who boat owner Bob Brown had hired to do something he couldn't or didn't want to do—catch the swordfish and then exchange it for treasure. The relationship worked as well as it did because trust, communication, and great alignment of goals existed on both ends. Bob didn't skimp on a seaworthy and well-equipped boat, and Dad maximized his skill set and resources to benefit the boat owner, the crew, and himself. Since everyone's paycheck was based on a percentage of the catch, more fish in the hold meant everyone was happy.

Just as on the Andrea Gail, needs, goals, and planning dictate the approaches and outcomes when it comes to your financial well-being. That's why here at Beauport Financial, we believe that now more than ever is a time for leadership and a clear, process-driven direction. Although we are agnostic regarding any product solutions, we are passionately engaged in the sound-advice business. We tell folks that we aim to be the last and best planner or advisory firm they form a relationship with.

We follow a proven process (more about this in just a bit) that dictates the strategies employed, always keeping your best interests in mind, independent of any investment or insurance carrier, fund group, or home office. As previously mentioned, we are—and act—as fiduciaries, which means we put your best interests ahead of anyone else's. We let your plan dictate the solutions and strategies that are most prudent for implementation, and then set sail and monitor along the way. By doing so, we do our best to mitigate dangers—both known and unknown—as best we can, and have the plan for grounding purposes. If the plan hasn't changed and your priorities remain the same, then we stay the course.

Having created income streams for you in your retirement, we make sure to continue reviewing the overall picture with you two times a year, every year, in good times and bad. We still ask questions like:

- How did we do?
- Where are we according to your plan expectations?
- How did the financial markets perform?
- What are the dividends and interest?
- Is the original plan still viable?
- What do we need to change and why?

As we discussed in Chapter 6, we also keep looking at whether you need to continue taking market risk or whether you have enough to live the life you want and still leave a financial legacy. If a 6 percent return on accumulated assets will sail you into retirement with reduced risk, you may want to play it safer instead of positioning yourself for possible 9 to 10 percent returns and assuming that increased risk.

In short, we address both obstacles and opportunities as well as the estate, income, gifting, allocation, and risk protection issues that lurk above and below the waterline. We're going to talk a lot about that latter point in this chapter. First, however, we need to look at taxes.

Optimizing Your Tax Situation

When it comes to making your money really work for you as you near or enter retirement, it's all about being prepared. Nowhere does that hold truer than with taxes. That's why we never have you put all your money into a single barrel.

"Barrels?" you ask.

Let me explain.

When Dad was groundfishing commercially for cod, haddock, and flounder after he left the swordfishing industry, he'd always have a blue, 55-gallon plastic barrel with seawater in it on deck for the lobster by-catch. The lobsters weren't the targeted species, but they were undoubtedly welcomed by the crew who divvied them up to bring home to their families once they hit the docks. The barrel safeguarded this asset that would be enjoyed later on—just like assets being saved and invested for future enjoyment.

When it comes to investing the money you're saving for retirement, you don't just have that single, blue barrel in which to store your assets. You have three (more on this later) that can hold a limitless amount of assets. Now imagine that each barrel has a spigot on the bottom and that each barrel is taxed differently as the tap is turned on and the asset distributed out. Your objective is to strategically position your money in the three barrels to optimize both tax diversification as well as asset allocation (the percentage of stocks to bonds and the different kinds of stocks you have).

To say it another way, the name of the game when it comes to investing is to come up with a strategy that's advantageous during your earning years as well as your retirement. That's not an idea that gets a lot of press. Everything you see, read, and hear—even from financial professionals—focuses on accumulation planning:

- "Invest here."
- "Buy these funds."
- "Don't buy that."
- "Hold on to your stock."
- "Sell now."

While 99 percent of financial advice focuses on accumulating money, that's only part of the picture.

For starters, you want to make sure those retirement funds are working for you along the way. So many people come to me and say, "Well, hey, I'm 66—now I'm retiring. I don't want to take any risk. Just put my money in something that'll be protected." The problem with that thinking is that they're potentially going to be retired for 25 to 30 years, and if that money doesn't keep growing, they're going to outlive their retirement savings. By trying to play it safe and protect their money instead of allowing it to continue working for them, they're putting themselves at substantial financial risk.

You also want to make sure you can access your retirement funds in a tax-efficient manner when it's time to start dipping into all that money you've saved.

My dad sure knew that he had to think not just about catching the fish, but how he was going to distribute the fish in return for cash. Let's say he had a banner trip and filled the boat with 30,000 pounds of swordfish. Awesome! But really stupid if he sold the swordfish for $3 a pound in Gloucester when he could have taken the fish to Boston, which is an hour away by boat, and gotten $5 a pound. That's a difference of $60,000.

Similarly, you don't want to be giving away big money when some pre-planning could prevent that. And that gets us back to those three barrels that started this whole conversation.

- Barrel #1 is a taxable account that contains brokerage accounts, savings and checking accounts, CDs, trust accounts, shares of stock you might hold directly, etc. We pretty much all have Barrel #1. If you have any kind of interest-bearing checking account or a savings account, you'll get a 1099 from the bank and have to pay the government a piece of those earnings. Even though any interest or dividend income you earn from the money in Barrel #1 gets taxed every April 15th, you'll wind up getting taxed a second time should you sell those holdings at a gain. So why put anything in Barrel #1? Because that's where you access the liquid funds you need to live on, as well as those three to six months of emergency living expenses sitting in the bank. Since there are no restrictions on when you can use the money in Barrel #1, you'll also want to stash surplus cash there. But that doesn't mean you have to keep this portion of Barrel #1 in the bank. While you don't care how low the interest rate is on the emergency expenses you've squirreled away, anything above that should be working for you. So, you need

to be out fishing in more fruitful waters, looking for that 3 to 6 percent instead of settling for the interest the bank is paying.
- Barrel #2 is a tax-deferred account. Think traditional IRAs, traditional 401Ks, pension plans, and the like. The money you put in this barrel lowers your taxable income for that year, and any growth remains tax-deferred until those funds are distributed during your retirement. You'll have to pay tax on anything you take out of that account when you retire, but since you likely won't be working by that point, there's a good chance you'll fall into a lower tax bracket. On the other hand, who knows what the tax rate will be then.
- Barrel #3 is a tax-free account that can include Roth IRAs or Roth 401ks, along with 529 plans for your kids, cash value life insurance, and income from some municipal bonds. Although you receive no tax deduction while funding the account (so the amount you contribute to the fund is still included in that year's taxable income), as long as you don't tap it for five years or before you're 59 ½ years old, that's the last tax you (or your heirs) will pay not only on the money you contributed but on any growth your investment has generated. In short, it not only accumulates tax-free but it's also distributed tax-free. So, whenever money comes out of that barrel, it's coming out as a whole dollar with no tax implications at all. Talk about a win-win!

Your choice of which barrel to put your money into is dictated by how you want that money taxed while it sits in that account and how it's going to be taxed on the way out the door, whether the funds are being tapped by you or your heirs.

Many folks lean on the first two barrels instead of filling the third barrel in order to take advantage of tax savings now. But tax-free money in retirement or as a legacy asset is a beautiful thing, especially if tax rates are the same or higher in retirement than they were when you were earning. So, planning a way to fund a tax-free income asset for later years in retirement can be a great strategy.

Say you decide that you need $50,000 a year once you quit working. You can take that $50,000 from a single barrel, but that may wind up costing you big on the tax front. Or perhaps you're transitioning into retirement and need to supplement part-time earned income. Your financial planner's job is to figure out the best barrels to use in order to get that $50,000 to you in a tax-efficient way. Down the line, decisions about which barrel to draw from may even be impacted by a desire to reduce your heirs' future tax liability. Regardless, having all three barrels sufficiently filled gives you multi-pronged options on the tax front, and that can be a real blessing.

This is probably a good time to remind ourselves of the obvious. A successful retirement journey doesn't start the day you decide to retire. That groundwork was set years before, when you built the boat, considered the destination, chose the crew, came up with the navigation plan, and invested in the supplies before even pushing off the dock. So, if you're still in the pre-retirement, accumulation phase of your life, you might want to give some serious consideration to that often-neglected Barrel #3.

My wife and I even introduced our working teenage children to this opportunity by offering to match their $250 contribution to a Roth IRA. We got the ball rolling in the hopes of enticing the kids to invest, and it worked. They can add their own funds to the account up to the maximum $7,000 per year. To fund a Roth in 2024, your adjusted gross income has to be less than $146,000 as an individual ($240,000 if you're filing joint returns), so that's not exactly a problem for our kids.

To help convince them to participate in funding their Roth IRAs, we explained what Einstein called the eighth wonder of the world—compound interest (that's when you earn interest on your interest)—along with the Rule of 72. Take your expected rate of return and divide it into 72 to get the number of years it takes for money being compounded to double. For example, an 8 percent return would take nine years to double since eight goes into 72 nine times (72 ÷ 8 = 9).

Right then and there, our 18-year-old did the math and realized that the $500 (250 of his, 250 of ours) at an 8 percent rate of return would double in value every nine years, so at 72 years of age that initial sum could be worth $32,000 tax-free. Talk about compelling math and a powerful message, especially since we offered to match funds every year.

We made a point to provide our children with financial guidance, but the fact is that we all need those insights to help us take stock. And that boils down to finding the right professional to partner with.

The Retirement Game Plan

Timing, chemistry, and clear expectations are the key ingredients to a solid and productive relationship. All of this might as well be addressed up front, so no one has to guess along the way. Finances and money trigger emotion and memories—some great, some bad. As a financial planner, I have to recognize that fact, along with my clients' diverse economic backgrounds. Most people do not get unhappy with their advisor until they hit rough seas, and lack of information or miscommunication breeds contempt, anxiety, or high emotions that can lead to a decision crisis right in the middle of a storm.

You can't afford to have that happen.

In the years leading up to retirement, you've assessed and made modifications as you fished. You set out for that sweet fishing spot, followed a process, adapted as you went along, and reeled in the treasures. Once you hit retirement and you're no longer fishing, however, everything changes. As soon as you retire, you're no longer earning and saving portions of your earned income. No paycheck, no salary deferring, no contribution to your IRA or 401k. Now you're spending what you have already saved. So, it's critically important to have a game plan in place before you retire.

That starts with taking stock of what you have by answering three questions as you enter—or near—retirement:

1. Do you have a lifetime income plan?
2. Do you have a tax strategy? Because let's not forget that you have a silent business partner in retirement, called

the IRS. They want their 15–25 percent or more. If a client tells me they need $60,000 a year, that means I need to generate about $80,000 gross. How much do *you* need to generate? You won't know until you sit down and look at the numbers.

3. Do you have a protection plan (i.e., insurance)?

These are critical questions because the only way to avoid blowing it is to have a solid game plan. That's how Betsy, an out-of-state client, handled her retirement.

To be honest, Betsy's game plan didn't materialize all at once. She was forced into coming up with the first part of her plan when she lost her husband in 2015. Knowing that she would need money, she immediately sold their vacation home in Georgia to replace some of the lost income and to minimize expenses.

"I'm not going back there," she said. "I've got my property here in Illinois."

That helped her with the financial piece.

Six months before her retirement date, she had already figured out the rest of the game plan.

"I realize that I'm going to have at least 40 hours a week of extra time," she told me. "There are two local charities, one being a local library, that I want to get more involved in. And there are places in this country I'd like to see." Then she mentioned a local women's group she planned to meet up with for coffee more consistently. Knowing what she wanted her life to look like allowed her to formulate the game plan that would allow her to make that life happen.

Most people don't talk about this pre-retirement preparation phase, let alone take steps to prepare for it. You get to it when you get to it. But it's critical to plan ahead of pushing off the dock on your final financial journey. No matter what your retirement looks like, it's going to be hard to adapt to the change if you haven't evaluated what you're adapting to. That's the only way you're going to wrap your brain around your new life. And it's likely the only way you're going to be able to afford it.

Betsy didn't try to scope out her entire retirement. That would have been impossible. But by planning out the first six months based on a candid self-assessment, she got a running start at it and will avoid some of the pitfalls that so many retirees encounter. In six months, we'll re-evaluate once stuff has come up, as it always does.

Watch Out for Assumptions

The only way to know if it's time to retire is to define what financial success means to you. My dad was very clear about what made for a successful trip:

- The least possible number of days at sea—17 days was his fastest dock-to-dock expedition.
- Good weather.
- Boat safety and security.
- Lots of fish.
- A good price at the dock.

- A quick turnaround once in port that came from taking stock as Dad steamed home.
- And not forgetting anything important. You can't run short on hooks or bait or engine oil out at sea without significant time and money implications. Thorough preparation was key.

When he planted the seed with his crew to inspire them to achieve all that, he would say, "Hey, guys, here's how we're going to have a kick-ass trip. We get out there, we catch a bunch of fish, we load the hold, we get our asses back, we sell it, we come back out, and we're home in, like, three weeks. The flip side is that we waste time, we're last in line when we get out there, and we've missed the full moon to boot. As a result, we're out way too long, we get back last, and we only get three and a half or four bucks a pound as opposed to five since there's now a glut of fish on the market."

Dad's clarity about what entailed success, and what he had to do to and/or change to achieve it, allowed him to provide for himself, his family, and his crew.

So how do you define success? Maybe it's living long enough to enjoy the fruits of your labor and then ensuring when you're gone, the assets and lessons don't go with you, a concept we'll talk about in the next chapter. Whatever your definition, creating a financial plan, implementing that plan, monitoring that plan, and then finally taking stock of where you're at in the big picture are all critical to help ensure that you wind up where you want to be in your retirement years.

This is not the time to make assumptions—either about market performance or about your longevity. While you have the ability to save and invest, that's about the only thing you can dictate. You certainly can't control the market or the sequence of returns and how that impacts your retirement savings should the market go into recession.

But you can hedge your bet by making sure that you're not allowing expectations to influence your retirement-related game plan, since those suppositions can all too often prove to be flawed. That's what happened to Holmes and Elicia.

At the time I met Holmes, he was the oldest living male in his family. Since not a single male in his lineage had made it to 60 years, he somewhat logically assumed that he, too, would die prematurely. Figuring that he would experience early mortality, he retired young and then tapped his Social Security early to enjoy whatever remained of his life. He loved jazz and had an amazing record collection of old jazz musicians, so he and his wife attended jazz festivals around the country. Their zest for travel also led them to take several cruises. Eager to also enjoy their home when not on the road, they took out a second mortgage in order to renovate their kitchen, put in new windows, and fence the yard. They even added an in-ground pool because they wanted to see their five grandkids, who, as expected, subsequently came to visit more frequently.

Ironically, ten years after retiring, Holmes was still chugging right along and was still relatively healthy. That was great news except for one thing. Having lived longer than anticipated, he had pretty much run through his retirement funds. As it turns out, they wound up with enough money to continue funding their lifestyle, but only because he was fortunate and inherited some money. But without a plan, he could have easily spent that windfall as well.

I'm guessing that's why they came to have a conversation. Holmes's wife, Elicia, a teacher who was just a little bit older than Holmes and whose mom had lived to be in her 90s, was concerned about her husband's penchant for spending money. Although she was still working part-time to stay mentally sharp and socially engaged, and although she had a guaranteed pension, Elicia knew they needed a game plan that would satisfy her husband's need to live large while making sure that he didn't blow through their savings.

"Don't show me living to 80, that's nuts," Holmes said when we met to discuss the financial plan I developed for them.

Elicia countered, "You better show us living to 90, or I'm not signing off on the plan."

Clearly, I would have to devise a plan that satisfied some very different priorities. I came up with a retirement income plan that Elicia could endorse, and that still allowed Holmes to indulge his spirit of adventure by creating a travel/entertainment barrel with a $15,000-a-year budget funded by the dividends generated by his inheritance. Since he was still healthy enough to get life insurance, that also was part of the game plan, a financial strategy we'll discuss later in this chapter.

The couple's game plan ensured that their retirement could be adequately funded. Before we had that in place, however, their golden years were starting to look downright tarnished.

Reality Check

The only real guarantee you can count on in retirement is that you'll need a little more money each year if for no other reason than inflation, as prices do go up. As we've discussed, life happens. You have to mitigate the risk you know about as well as the risk you don't, all while preparing for the things you want to do. That only comes with taking stock and making an assessment.

Who's going to do that?

That's your financial captain's job.

It's not easy to tell people what they don't want to hear. But a good advisor needs to tell folks what needs to be said and done, whether or not the client will be happy with the news. That's why I had to challenge one of my clients a few years back.

Divorcee Cindy's penchant for cars had prompted her to buy a new one every three to four years. That would have been fine if she could have afforded all those shiny vehicles with that new-car smell. But she couldn't.

"I can't help myself," Cindy said when I suggested she hold off. "I'm a magnet to car dealerships. Every 36 to 48 months, I've got to get something new."

I knew that's what she had done when she was married. But she was no longer part of a two-income household. Someone had to hit her between the eyes, and that someone was me.

"Well, you're spending too much," I said. "If you continue to spend 15 percent of your account every year, you'll be broke in seven years."

She didn't love hearing that at first, but a year later, she thanked me.

"No one ever pointed that out," she said, admitting that her husband had fueled the spending engine that kept chugging right along after her divorce.

In the end, our exchange cemented a healthy relationship as well as a bond of trust between us. It also prompted her to redo her budget and forgo buying a new car every three years.

Taking Stock
It bears repeating—habits, good or bad, are hard to break. If you're used to buying that new car every three to four years, you're not going to want to keep driving your old one, especially when it seems like you have a lot of money tucked away. But indulging your spending habits, even if you're not buying big-ticket items, can add up over time without you even realizing it. That's why you need those financial checkups, just like you need to see your doctor for that physical every year. And sometimes, the doc is going to call you on something that doesn't seem like a big deal but could become one.

Five years ago, I headed in for my annual physical. When I jumped on the scale, I was three pounds heavier than I had been the year before.

Who cares about three pounds, right? But the doctor put that in perspective.

"Derek, not a big deal," he said. "But if you gain three pounds a year for the next ten years, you're gonna weigh 210 pounds, and your frame can't support 210 pounds."

Financial excesses add up the same way those few pounds here and there do. To make sure you're okay, you have to figure out where you're at and how your current spending levels are going to impact your future bottom line. That extra couple percent you're taking every year doesn't seem like a big deal until you're 80, and there's nothing left. Then it's one heck of a big deal.

So, you have to stay on top of things and take stock.

In Dad's business, taking stock could be as simple as figuring out that if they had left a day earlier, they would have wound up being first or second in line instead of fifth, an important distinction when it came to how much fish they would catch.

In my business, taking stock means monitoring a client's progress vis-à-vis the financial goals that have been set. I sit down with people who have $2 million-plus and are worried about taking an extra trip or joining the golf club or joining the yacht club or are concerned about spending $80,000 a year when their portfolio is up $145,000 in a year.

"Look, you're 70-something years old," I'll tell them. "If you take a 5 percent distribution every year, that's $100,000 on $2 million. Right now, you're averaging a 6 percent return. At this rate, by the time you're in your 80s and 90s, you're going to wind up with even more than $2 million."

That's a pretty easy conversation to have. The one I had with Cindy is less so. But as a financial captain, I can't just run and hide and avoid the obvious, or only communicate when times are good to note the positive returns on your quarterly performance reports. The only way to know if your financial plan remains viable or needs to change is for your financial advisor to keep score and then share that information with you.

Keeping score isn't just about dollars and cents. It can't be. You can't just look at your statement and say, "Oh, I made money." While that's great, that's not the full story. You have to be accountable not just for what you've accumulated, but also for what you're spending. Also, you have to think about how much risk you're assuming.

If my dad had come back after an average trip but was five days late having blown through three hydraulic lines or burned a ton of extra fuel after taking the boat into places that he shouldn't have been, that would have cut into the revenue. And in the long run, it wouldn't have benefitted anybody.

Keeping score can't be just about the numbers, because what you need to know is whether you need to pull back and play it a bit safer. You need to look at it and ask yourself, "Well, if I'm doing okay because I own these emerging market bonds that happen to have had a good quarter, but on a scale of 1 to 10, they're an 11 from a risk standpoint, can I afford to keep doing that?"

Sure, you might get lucky once or twice or even more, but that kind of speculative investing gets people in trouble. We saw that in 2001 with the dot-com bubble, in 2008-2009 with the mortgage crisis, and again in 2022 with tech companies in a rising-interest-rate world.

Risk Protection
As the saying goes, it's better to be lucky than good, but you can't count on that. You have to do your part. You have to plan right, stick to the plan, monitor as you go, assess what's working and what's not, and do what's necessary to protect your assets. The latter is also part of taking stock. That's why, during every review, we talk about risk mitigation strategies.

While the topic of risks associated with retirement can be something of a downer, it doesn't have to be, especially if you plan right. For example, you certainly don't want to deplete a significant portion of your assets should you fall ill or become disabled. By factoring long-term care and disability insurance planning into your risk-mitigation strategy, you'll be able to withdraw money for your living expenses, knowing that you're covered if things suddenly take a turn and go south.

I hate to be the one to tell you this, but there's a pretty good likelihood that will happen. Let's face it, mortality is 100 percent guaranteed. We don't like to think about it, but that's a given. A 2023 study conducted by A Place for Mom reveals that 70 percent of American adults 65 years or older are going to need some form of long-term health care. We don't like to think about that either, but that's also a reality. The very wealthy can self-fund this type of expensive care. The financially indigent get Medicaid when this unthinkable reality hits. But the majority of upper-middle-class millionaires have to hedge somehow. At Beauport, we use hybrid and combo life and long-term care rider life policies to address the need. Although these kinds of policies can be pricey, sometimes the taxable dividends from a trust or brokerage account are sufficient to cover the premiums. Even if that's not the case, leaving yourself financially exposed to a one-in-two chance that you'll get hit with a health challenge that could exhaust a chunk of your life savings is simply unthinkable.

Insuring the Money Machine
Just as you can protect yourself against those potentially debilitating medical expenses, you can help ensure that your annual post-retirement income doesn't take a terminal hit by investing in another kind of risk protection.

Aside from Social Security, 80+ percent of today's retirees do not have a government or income annuity to rely on for predictable lifetime income. If that describes you, listen up. You can use a piece of your private assets to create something that acts like a personal pension with a lifetime income guarantee. Using a reasonably expensed income annuity with a life benefit to supplement your retirement income can help fund essential lifestyle needs. This works because when the markets sink or a recession hits, you don't want to be forced to sell stocks that have taken a nosedive to finance your daily needs.

Whether you are fortunate enough to have retired with a pension or decide to create one for yourself, however, that pension will only last as long as you do. That's okay if you're not married and have no family you want to provide for after your death or legacy you want to leave. The rest of us, however, should be looking at pension recovery insurance—life insurance purchased on the pension holder to replace all or a piece of the pension when they pass on.

Let's say you're lucky enough to retire with a $70,000 pension. To generate that kind of investment income, you would need to have $1.5 to $2 million in assets. That's a big deal! If you had a machine in the basement kicking out $70,000 a year of income, you damn well would insure it. Well, you're that machine. If you're healthy enough to qualify, you can take some of that $70,000 of guaranteed income and buy a life insurance policy. It won't be cheap, but you're spending dimes and quarters to get dollars' worth of benefits and to make sure that if you die too soon, the pension you're drawing is going to be replaced by a tax-free lump-sum life insurance policy that your spouse, your kids, and/or the trust are going to inherit.

Here's the kicker. Once the pension recovery piece kicks in via a tax-free lump sum death benefit paid to the beneficiary, these proceeds can be invested, which provides an annual income stream. So, you can essentially keep the income train going even from the grave. Talk about resting easy, knowing that your loved ones will be cared for after you go—or that you've left a life-defining legacy, which we'll talk more about in the next chapter.

Life Insurance Basics

As you can see, life insurance can play a significant role in financial planning. So, let's take a quick look at how it works beyond replacing a pension.

Life insurance comes in two flavors. Term life is called "term" because it's good for a set term of years—usually 10, 15, or 20—and then expires or renews at much higher rates on an annual basis. Permanent life or cash value life coverage, if funded correctly and designed right, will last until mortality (hence permanency of coverage) and allows you to access your cash in the policy on a tax-free basis during your lifetime if you opt to cancel it and get your premium dollars back. There are many kinds of permanent insurance policies (universal, variable, whole life, etc.), and all allow for your build-up of cash to be either used during your lifetime or provide the lasting coverage that will not expire before you do.

Let me clarify the difference between the two main life insurance categories. Think about auto insurance. You pay it every year, and even if you never get in an accident, you don't get any of your money back. So, if you pay $1,000 annually over the next 20 years, and you never get in a car accident, you're out $20,000. That's how term coverage works. Say you're 35 years old, you don't smoke, and you're a female. The cost of a term life insurance policy might be 400 bucks a year for a half-million dollars of coverage for 20 years. That's peanuts. But the actuaries have figured out that if you're healthy, 35, don't smoke, and aren't diabetic, the chances of you dying between 35 and 55 are so minuscule that they're most likely going to collect $8,000 in premiums from you until you're 56. At that point, you'll have to buy another policy. Since you'll be a lot older at that point, it's going to be more expensive. And even then, you could easily outlive that term life insurance policy.

By contrast, a correctly designed and funded permanent insurance contract for which you pay $1,000 a year is going to pay out since you're definitely going to die. However, the death benefit will be substantially less for the same premium compared to term insurance. While you won't personally recoup the money since you'll be gone, your beneficiary will. But this isn't just a dollar-for-dollar savings account. Over the course of that 20 years, part of that monthly premium you pay gets invested, so that initial death benefit may increase too.

But what if you want to use that money while you're still alive? You can because, unlike term life insurance, permanent life insurance typically has an actual cash value. The cash value element of permanent life insurance—whether whole life variable or universal life insurance—is a tax-free living benefit that, when distributed correctly, you can access and use. There's a catch, however. If you distribute all the policy's cash value, then you no longer have a death benefit or life insurance coverage, so any gain on the money from the policy that you cashed in is now ordinary income taxable. Not a great idea tax-wise, and you've now lost all your life insurance. So, care needs to be taken when accessing your tax-favored living benefit stored up in cash-value life insurance programs.Still, permanent life insurance can be an advantageous tool for tax-free accumulation. If the insured passes before retirement, the death benefit is paid as a lump sum that can't be taxed. If the policy owner lives long enough to enjoy the tax-favored accumulation built up inside the policy, tax-free income payments can be designed that act as a form of premium recovery plus gains on investment made. So, this winds up being another way to accumulate wealth and a potential third barrel tax-deferred, tax-free asset that can be viewed as a more expensive Roth IRA or Roth 401k with a death benefit.

Permanent life insurance is more expensive than a term policy. Still, you're investing in yourself rather than just paying that monthly premium as you do with your auto insurance premium. To use another analogy, it's like renting versus owning. The cost of home ownership is a lot higher, but you're building up equity in the house, and it's yours.

Protecting the Catch
Just as you shield yourself and your loved ones against income loss and catastrophic expenses, you can make sure that all of your retirement savings don't get wiped out in a storm by playing it safe on the investment front.

Mistakes can happen all along the journey toward retirement, but as you get closer, the errors are compounded and get a lot bigger. That makes sense. If you make a mistake while you're still fishing, the loss burns, but you can recover by continuing to fish. If you make it after you've gotten all your fish on the boat and are looking to cash in, instead of getting sunburned, you could wind up torching the entire catch and even the boat. Remember, the catch is only as good as getting it back to shore safely along with the boat and the crew so you can turn it into money.

Unfortunately, mistakes can and do happen on the way home. Oh shoot, we don't have enough fuel. Or we have an engine down. So, this is the time when you need to say, "Okay, I got what I was fishing for. What do I do with it? How do I take it? What do I turn it into? How do I protect it?"

At Beauport, we use a RISK™ blueprint, also known as our Retirement Income Survival Kit, to define and align your assets for income generation and asset protection. In addition to outlining strategies on a number of fronts, including estate planning, life insurance, and long-term care planning, the blueprint identifies which barrels, which we talked about earlier in this chapter, will provide maximum income leverage so we can replace earned income with investment income. It also arranges the investments you've been accumulating over the years for retirement according to your income needs, and is designed so that if you need 5–7 percent returns long-term in order not to outlive your assets, you're fishing in the right waters to accomplish that without running any unnecessary risk.

In addition, the RISK™ blueprint identifies whether you have the necessary built-in safeguards when it comes to asset allocation. If you invest too much money, say 20 percent of your portfolio, in international stocks and that 20 percent tanks, you could potentially not recover from the downturn if you're nearing or in retirement. We want to make sure that doesn't happen.

As we've seen, a certain amount of risk is part and parcel of investing. But it bears repeating that if all of your retirement savings could be wiped out in a storm, it's my role to say, "Hey, you've got $1 million here, why don't we take $300,000 of that and guarantee a 5 percent income stream using a more expensive but guaranteed income annuity. We'll protect the remaining $700,000 as much as we can with diversification, but no matter what, that $300,000 annuity is going to pay you $15,000 a year, which amounts to $1,250 bucks a month. So, it winds up being much like another guaranteed Social Security check you can't outlive, and it's safe no matter what happens to the market."

Ultimately, however, risk protection and successful course corrections depend on having a couple of contingencies in your back pocket should things not go according to plan, another lesson Dad taught me.

Dad and me in 2024.

Contingency Plan

When you're out at sea, you have to consider your engine and equipment, and then be prepared to adapt no matter what happens. That includes having a fallback so that when the ice machine breaks, because it will, you not only have the tools on board to fix it along with someone who knows how to use those tools, you've already purchased 50 percent of the ice you need from the Cape Pond Ice Company before leaving. Having two-and-a-half feet of ice on the floor of the hold pens to make sure the treasured catch never touches the hold's concrete floor where lingering bacteria might negatively impact the quality was a tiny but vital price to ensure a good payday. Did that sometimes mean throwing ice overboard to make room for the fish? Absolutely. But, as Captain Charlie would say, frozen water is cheap, but the fish is expensive.

Dad realized that he almost always needed to be working on Plan B or C instead of his original Plan A because he knew that there would never be a straight line to success.

With finances, contingency planning is equally paramount, primarily because all our projections are based on averages, which are impacted year to year by how your investments perform in the market or how much money you might need in a particular period. As we know, storms happen, and sometimes Plan B is forced upon you. All the planning in the world will always be trumped by a rotten health diagnosis or unfortunate life event.

Matt and Joyce, professionals in their late 60s, seemed like they were home-free on the financial front. Not only had they paid off the mortgage on their primary home, but they had also covered the university educations for all their children while still managing to consistently save and invest for retirement. In addition to investing in their 401ks and establishing a joint brokerage account, they had put aside a year's worth of living expenses just in case something unexpected happened.

Saving money for retirement had been the goal. Unfortunately, Joyce and Matt were unprepared from an insurance protection standpoint. Their asset levels were great, but when Matt unexpectedly was stricken with a crippling, terminal illness that rendered him unable to continue his career, they had no risk protection in place.

They had to adapt to his Category 5 storm since the diagnosis indicated that his already compromised health was quickly going to deteriorate even further. If he made it to retirement age, the costs for his care would soon escalate, even if Joyce stopped working full-time—or altogether—to help out with doctors' appointments, therapy sessions, and generally offer tender loving care as things started to change for the worse.

That's the problem with only focusing on Plan A.

You can spend all your time concentrating on Plan A and be forced into emergency mode when the financial seas get rough. In practical terms, that could mean being forced to sell investments at a loss or having to scramble on the financial front when confronted with a crisis like what Matt and Joyce experienced. On the other hand, if you've spent time developing Plans B, C, and D, not only will you not have to turn those paper losses into real ones, but you'll probably also have extra cash on hand with which to buy a bunch of shares on sale.

Regrettably, Joyce and Matt hadn't focused on a contingency plan. Knowing full well that they needed a new game plan, and the sooner, the better, the couple's estate planner introduced my partner and me to these nice folks. Most of their investments, it turned out, were held in accounts at a 1-800 brokerage firm with no advisor. So instead of having an actual investment plan in place, they were heavily invested in stocks with lots of downside risk. The money on paper looked great—the result of great saving habits and a favorable long-term run in go-go growth stocks. Thank goodness for that! They could have been a lot worse off financially speaking. But with no safety net, one setback would have compromised their ability to pay for Matt's healthcare and would have prevented Joyce from retiring early—or at all—to help her husband.

Our solution was to have them use their cash reserve funds to help offset future healthcare costs. Since we knew that Joyce and Matt would have to use significant retirement assets early to fund expected daily care needs once that ran dry, we came up with a significant redo of their portfolios, reducing the asset allocation risk that was primarily weighted to tech stocks. Our RISK™ blueprint and investment planning process did wonders to minimize the unknowns regarding what the assets could provide at an earlier-than-expected drawdown. That income planning provided Joyce with the tangible and reliable assurance that she would be able to retire early to help her spouse in the health and life battle they were about to face together.

So sure, you'll want to try to keep Plan A going strong, even as you work on Plan B or C, should you have to throw Plan A out the window and adapt. That way if Plan B or Plan C wind up having to take the place of Plan A, you'll be ready. And you may even find that Plan B winds up working out better than Plan A. When you plan for 7 percent returns and get 9 percent returns, for example, you treat yourself to that new car, extend the family trip, or do whatever else floats your boat.

Preparing for the Storms Ahead

Even when we do a whole lot of things right, life doesn't always work out the way we'd planned. Matt and Joyce have a home and have assets. With dual high incomes, they were on a trajectory for even more significant retirement savings. A single diagnosis took a lot of that away, so Plan B had to be incorporated out of necessity.

What's your Plan B? Have you got one just in case, or are you working toward one?

From disabilities to death or divorce, to business layoffs or closings, life can take us on a screwball journey. No straight lines. (Remember that?) So, you must put contingency plans in place when it comes to investing. As we've discussed, your financial planning must account for the fact that there are things in our control and external factors happening all around us that are always out of our control, including recessions, corrections, global expansions, interest rates, economic cycles, earnings reports, upcoming elections, and the political process, to name just a few. So, part of adaptation includes assessing what you can control and creating contingency plans for the rest. It doesn't matter what an average return is. No one hits that average in a linear fashion. And that yo-yo sequence of returns at the end of your years could spell disaster.

Imagine this if you will:

> *It's 2007. You make a critical financial decision to retire and live on your Social Security check and income from your 401k plan, which, after 30 years of hard work and exercising the excellent habit of paying yourself first, you've*

maxed. Since your employer has matched all your contributions to your 401k, you're sitting on the small mountain of assets needed to fund your lifestyle. So, you begin to collect your monthly Social Security pension and create a game plan for drawing down income from the retirement portfolio. It all sounds great, Then, wham! The Great Recession of 2008 begins with banks and mortgage companies failing. By the end of the blood bath, your nest egg has shrunk by 20–30 percent at a time when you're in the distribution phase of life instead of the contribution/accumulation phase. As you can see from the chart below, the sequence of your returns has everything to do with whether your money will last. Knowing that isn't helping your state of mind. Things get so bad that you're afraid to open up your monthly statements to see the paper losses on your account balances. You're beside yourself in anger, frustration, and fear regarding what could be next.

What do you do? Should you do anything at all? What are the pundits saying on television—in or out, buy or sell, optimism or pessimism, hold tight, or this time it's different? Why even care about what they're saying since they all contradict each other?

Things are crazy and moving fast. All signs point to further economic collapse. Will another big financial institution go belly up over a weekend as Lehman Brothers did? What if the market goes down 10 percent for the second year in a row? You can't have all your money at risk since you need to be able to draw on it.

Steaming Back Home & Taking Stock 223

CHART 1 - LUCKY INVESTOR "UP" MARKET				CHART 2 - UNLUCKY INVESTOR "DOWN" MARKET			
Age	Annual Return	Annual Withdrawal	Year-End Value	Age	Annual Return	Annual Withdrawal	Year-End Value
65			$ 800,000	65			$ 800,000
66	5%	$ 48,000	$ 792,000	66	-22%	$ 48,000	$ 567000
67	28%	$ 48,000	$ 965,760	67	-12%	$ 48,000	$ 458,880
68	22%	$ 48,000	$ 1,130,227	68	-9%	$ 48,000	$ 369,581
69	-5%	$ 48,000	$ 1,025,715	69	17%	$ 48,000	$ 384,409
70	38%	$ 48,000	$ 1,367,487	70	22%	$ 48,000	$ 420,979
71	19%	$ 48,000	$ 1,579,310	71	6%	$ 48,000	$ 398,238
72	23%	$ 48,000	$ 1,894,551	72	-15%	$ 48,000	$ 290,503
73	9%	$ 48,000	$ 2,017,061	73	9%	$ 48,000	$ 268,648
74	31%	$ 48,000	$ 2,594,350	74	14%	$ 48,000	$ 258,258
75	23%	$ 48,000	$ 3,143,050	75	25%	$ 48,000	$ 274,823
76	34%	$ 48,000	$ 4,163,687	76	14%	$ 48,000	$ 265,298
77	-26%	$ 48,000	$ 3,033,129	77	5%	$ 48,000	$ 230,563
78	-15%	$ 48,000	$ 2,530,159	78	-15%	$ 48,000	$ 147,979
79	5%	$ 48,000	$ 2,608,667	79	-26%	$ 48,000	$ 61,504
80	14%	$ 48,000	$ 2,925,881	80	34%	$ 48,000	$ 34,416
81	25%	$ 48,000	$ 3,609,351	81	23%	$ 42,332	$ 0
82	14%	$ 48,000	$ 4,066,660	82	31%		
83	9%	$ 48,000	$ 4,384,659	83	9%		
84	-15%	$ 48,000	$ 3,678,961	84	23%		
85	6%	$ 48,000	$ 3,851,698	85	19%		
86	22%	$ 48,000	$ 4,651,072	86	38%		
87	17%	$ 48,000	$ 5,393,754	87	-5%		
88	-9%	$ 48,000	$ 4,860,316	88	22%		
89	-12%	$ 48,000	$ 4,229,078	89	28%		
90	-22%	$ 48,000	$ 3,250,681	90	5%		
	8%		$ 3,250,681		8%		

The visual display above shows how sequence of return can affect your investments. The lucky investor returns are inverse compared to the unlucky investor. The returns shown are hypothetical and for illustrative purposes only.

Too many people entering retirement in 2007 and 2008 experienced the above scenario. And while that recession was, in a word, extreme, we know that others will follow. We just don't know when.

Author and speaker Andy Andrews says, "You're either coming out of a storm, getting through a storm presently, or heading into a future storm." That's life. So you need to understand the risks involved in the accumulation stage (for Dad, that included the hunt for—and the harvesting of—fish) as well as the distribution and legacy stage (getting the crew, boat, and catch back to the dock safely to reap the reward) of the retirement journey, and then assess where you are on the spectrum and how best to handle the situation. This ability to adapt is essential for your financial health and well-being, and for creating the retirement you've always dreamed of.

Setting the Stage for a Great Retirement

What makes for a great retirement? Everyone's dream retirement is going to be different, but one thing we can all agree on—we want to have a plan in place that allows us to realize that dream, whatever it is. And, as we've seen, that starts early. Just as Captain Charlie prepped the boat and crew ahead of leaving port to increase the chances of a successful sword trip, a dignified and independent retirement requires the same forethought on a number of fronts.

It's great that you've got a plan.

It's great that you adjust your budget.

It's great that you adjust your timeline because you're living longer or you intend to live longer, or because you have already lived longer than any family member.

But are you ready mentally and emotionally? You probably won't know that answer until you're in retirement since you've never done it before. So how the heck are you supposed to anticipate how this new part of your life is going to go? Once again, making that determination requires an assessment.

Joe Trovato, a colleague from Bakersfield, California, who is part of a financial advisors' study group I belong to, works with recent retirees from the oil and agriculture industries. When he realized that a lot of his male clients were struggling with the sudden lifestyle change related to trading their careers for a life of leisure, he started a men's group to help them through this new transition. Twice a year, they meet in the back room of a bar with the TV on, drink craft beer, eat food, and talk about what it's like to be retired, along with what they're up to and how they keep staying connected and mentally healthy.

At one of the first get-togethers, Joe noticed that a guy he knew seemed particularly uptight. "What are you worried about?" he asked. "You've got three and a half million bucks."

"It's not about the money. I've got the money," the man answered, his eyes filling with tears. "Every day was tied up in my job, my business, and my connections. And now I just cut that off."

He hadn't just left a job. He had stepped away from the life he had known and loved for decades, and hadn't figured out how to carve out a new one.

If you decide to retire, you, too, will have to adapt to your new free time. You'll have to find out what speaks to your heart and gives you a sense of purpose. You'll also have to contend with how the social component of your life will shift. If you're married, you're suddenly going to be seeing a lot more of your spouse. If you're single, you may wind up spending an awful lot of time alone. Either can be a darn hard adjustment unless you've carved out a plan before that last day on the job.

In the previous chapter, we talked about how the evaluation of one's life and investments necessarily leads to course changes. My dad adapted to the weather, adapted to the crew, adapted to the engine failing, all while baiting the hooks and setting the lines that would catch the swordfish his livelihood depended on. Eventually, he took stock not just of each trip, but of swordfishing in general, decided that it was no longer worth the risk, and got out.

Similarly, you've made changes and adapted to the circumstances in front of you to make sure you're on target with creating the assets you will rely on during your retirement. But as you steam home after all those inevitable course adjustments, and after taking stock to make sure that you're using those assets you worked so hard to create—for a retirement income stream that you can't outlive—you want to start thinking about what you'll leave behind in the way of memories, stories, and your legacy. Ultimately, that's what creative and confident planning provides: the freedom to focus on gifting and philanthropy, knowing that the assets and values that outlive you will create quite the navigation template for the next generation.

CATCH OF THE DAY:

- There are no straight lines from here to there, especially in the journey of life. When life happens, you may need to alter course, which is why having contingency plans is so critical. Just remember, making those adjustments is not the end of the world. We are all on Plan B or C anyway, aren't we?
- Know what you're fishing for, and into which barrel you're going to stockpile that treasure—taxable, tax-deferred, or tax-free.
- Some things we can control, some things we can't. Dad couldn't control the weather or the price of fish at the dock. But he could control how safe the boat was. He protected himself as much as he could, which is what you need to do by putting into place different income streams and risk strategies.
- Monitor your investments and seek input from an assembled team of trusted advisors—financial, tax, and legal.

CHAPTER 8
THE WAKE BEHIND YOUR BOAT: YOUR LEGACY AND VALUES

WHAT'S YOUR BEST FINANCIAL PLAN? According to some, it's taking your last breath and having the final check bounce. But is that really how we want to die—or live for that matter? That certainly isn't the legacy my dad or I have in mind, and it's probably not the one you want either.

While we can't control what folks will say, think, or feel about us when we're gone, every life leaves clues. The behaviors we've modeled over the years—what we've said, how we've framed conversations, the choices we've made, the examples we set—reflect our value systems and beliefs, and create a vision of who we are and what we stand for. That's what generates those stories about us that remain, even after we're gone. That's the wake behind the boat. That's our legacy.

When people hear the term legacy, they think, *Oh, it's a business. It's the family house. It's a big yacht. It's an art collection.* Those assets certainly may be part of your legacy, but your legacy is so much more. It could be a place like the lake house my in-laws own, which has spawned so many stories and fun times, including campfires, fishing trips, waterskiing, and shared meals. It could be the children or grandchildren you've set on the path to success. It could be the talents and passions you've shared with those around you. And, yes, it can certainly include the money you pass down to your heirs. But your legacy is also defined by your charity, your philanthropy, the impact you've made, and the people you've touched.

More than 70 percent of people in this country give money to charity while they're alive. That's fantastic! But how many people leave a bequest to those charities they were supporting after they die?

Just 7 percent.

What if everybody who reads this book gets inspired and donates just 1 to 5 percent of their wealth to the causes they care about after they die? Think about the impact that would have!

It all comes back to fishing for me. If the fishing has been good over time, you can reserve all the captain's cuts—the best pieces—for yourself, and still share plenty of fish. You don't need to gorge yourself on every single primo filet of every single fish. How much do you really need in the freezer? How much do you need in your fridge? And how much do you need on your plate? If you've determined that everybody's plate is full and you've got plenty in reserve, then give some away and keep making an impact after you're gone.

Your legacy will far outlive you however it winds up being defined. So, in addition to protecting what you have worked so hard to accumulate, positioning it to work well, and then bestowing what is left to the next generation or charity, you need to figure out what you want to be remembered for when you pass on. In short, what was it all for and what did you leave behind in your wake? Your why will dictate how you define the meaning of success and should provide one of the cornerstones of your financial plan. Perhaps you want to set aside a percentage of your assets or a specific asset so that it continues to have a positive impact even after you're gone. Or perhaps you want to set up a life insurance policy that benefits your heirs.

That's what my aunt, who died of ovarian cancer, did. Since she had no children of her own, the death claim wound up financing her niece and nephew's college education and covered a vacation that brought the family together. On the trip they took, courtesy of my aunt, they looked up to the sky, sent her a kiss, and toasted her memory.

Of course, to be able to leave that kind of life-changing family legacy, you need to have committed to saving money from earned income. Only after intentionally planning for a confident, well-designed, and well-lived retirement can you begin to feel like you can be charitable to others, be those your family, your friends, or the nonprofit organizations you care about. That's what Ginger and Luke did.

Planning Ahead
While still in their 30s, Luke and Ginger made a conscious decision to save money and invest prudently. Early in their marriage—already aware of the importance of dollar-cost averaging, compound interest, and paying yourself first—

they sat down together to figure out a savings and retirement investment plan.

Having met at graduate school, they appreciated the value of education and wanted to make sure their children all attended top schools. So, they geared their initial investments in that direction, and sure enough, their kids were all able to afford the universities they wanted to go to.

As the years passed, Ginger and Luke remained true to their original decision to save rather than spend. When they outgrew their modest home, they decided to stay put and add onto it rather than buy a more expansive, pricier piece of property. All the while, they continued to support the charities they believed in. That, too, was important to them.

When Ginger decided to quit her job in order to start a consulting company, she and Luke invested in insurance to mitigate that income risk. Her gamble paid off, and she eventually sold the company for seven figures. That helped! Even then, rather than step away from the practices that had put them on an outstanding path to retirement, they continued to live on a lot less than they earned.

To instill values in their kids, once they entered adulthood, Luke and Ginger gave each one $15,000 annually—$5,000 to spend on themselves, $5,000 to invest, and $5,000 to give to charity. When their kids were ready to settle down, the couple helped them with down payments so they could get into their first homes. They also established a trust to make sure the kids are taken care of. They've even set up college funds for each of the grandkids, who are now in the picture, to ensure that they, too, have the means to go to any school they get accepted to.

In short, this couple sees the value of paying it forward.

But that's just the start. When Luke and Ginger hired Beauport for financial planning, we ascertained that they had an identifiable amount of surplus above and beyond what they needed for their kids and for themselves to live and travel, while still maintaining and enjoying their principal residence along with an additional property they had acquired. Once we knew that the couple, now in their 60s, would always be able to ride out any financial storms in retirement, we explored the philanthropy piece as a concept, first in terms of family and then charities. With their investments generating thousands every month, they're able to gift most of that and pass it on.

What's the Wake Behind You Going to Look Like?

Have you given any thought to not just where you're headed but ultimately what you may leave behind when your voyage is completed?

Ideally, once you have safely achieved your financial goals and you continue to enjoy the experiences and opportunities that proper planning has afforded you, it becomes less about what you have and more about securing a better future for those you care about most. And there are so many ways to achieve that. Say you're an 87-year-old with a million-dollar IRA account (good for you!) who must continue to take required minimum distributions from that asset to satisfy IRS requirements. In reality, you've already outlived normal life expectancy, so the chances that your portfolio will be significantly diminished or completely exhausted are small. In this case, it may make sense to talk to your financial planner about positioning your portfolio for the next generation of children and/or grandchildren who will inherit the asset. Longer-term potential for growth is better for heirs if you are not spending all the money—their runway is longer and will benefit from a less conservative stance with longer-term investments and more time to let those grow.

Or remember how my wife and I encouraged our children to invest by matching their Roth IRA contributions? Even if you haven't filled that third barrel that we talked about in Chapter 7, matching Roth IRA contributions could provide a tax-free inheritance for your heirs, and teaching them to invest will help set them up for the kind of life you want for them.

There are other ways to create a legacy—and not just for your heirs. Vickie, a retired schoolteacher with a heart that's as beautiful as her smile, decided she wanted her contributions to local and global communities to outlive her. While teaching didn't exactly fill the coffers, she received a family inheritance, which she was eager to use to make the world just a little bit better.

During one of our client meetings a few years back, Vickie brought up the fact that she was about to start receiving mandatory required minimum distributions from two separate IRA accounts since she was about to turn 70 ½. "I don't really need the money," she said, acknowledging that while she does a certain amount of traveling, she lives fairly modestly and receives a steady income stream from a trust her husband left her.

"Well, why don't we think about being philanthropic and gift it?" I asked. "You could consider using a part of your IRA required minimum distribution to fund a foundation-owned charitable gift life insurance policy. We'll design it so that you're not paying for it for the rest of your life—just over the next ten years. And we'll leverage that money so we more than double the value of your premium investment. You'll name the global charities you want us to send that tax-free money to upon your death.

Vickie loved that. A few years back, she had heard about a girls' school in Nepal, Kathmandu, which was started because, at the time, only the boys were receiving any kind of education. She quickly decided to sponsor a student there, something my wife and I subsequently agreed to do as well. Knowing her financial support of this charity, and others that she cares about around the world, wouldn't stop when she died made her happy. "A lump-sum, tax-free gift upon my death isn't such a bad thing, is it?" she said.

This huge impact that she'll make when she passes is all being funded by the required minimum distributions she didn't need. That's what fills Vickie's tank. It's part of what fills my tank. We're actively making a difference.

So many of us think about our post-working years as retiring from something. But if you plan correctly, you can retire to something. Maybe you're going to indulge a particular passion that's been back-burnered for too long. Maybe you're going to be part of your new grandbaby's life and provide daycare services three days a week. Maybe you're just going to indulge yourself and not worry about leaving an asset legacy. And that's just fine if that's your intentional income and asset plan.

The trick is finding out which course you'd like to stay on and honoring that. Some retirees would rather distribute the majority of their assets while they're still alive, whether the funds are used for their enjoyment or their family's, distributed to a charity, or all three. There's something inspirational about being around to experience the blessing your act of kindness bestows upon others. Surprisingly, however, that can backfire unless you think it through. Give property to someone who doesn't want to maintain it or be a landlord, and you haven't done them any favors unless they can sell it efficiently.

Compare that to my philanthropic client, Jackie, who set up a trust for charity. The last time we talked, we decided to take $15,000 from the dividends and interests being generated by this trust and hand that money over to a local nonprofit.

"Oh, and by the way, you're going to get a $15,000 charitable deduction for doing this," I told Jackie as I passed her the forms she would need to sign to make this happen. "Instead of you paying taxes on the gains, interest, and dividends, you'll be able to itemize this gift along with your other deductions as a charitable contribution."

Unlike her husband, Dan, who hasn't been able to enjoy the reaction to his generosity, Jackie will be able to witness the difference her money makes.

Taking Care of Business

Careful planning creates the kind of legacy that makes your gift(s) so worthwhile. Unfortunately, despite the best intentions, it doesn't always work out that way. The last thing any of us want to do is make life tougher for the people we care about by miscalculating a bequest. Leaving behind a mess—whether big or small—of scattered liquid and non-liquid assets and no directions can be even worse. Not only will your heirs not know what you intended, but the lack of clarity can also cause infighting. To help ensure that doesn't happen, you want to think of your legacy as a tidy, well-maintained, and meaning-filled estate that you will pass on to the next generation of family members or heirs, or to the causes you care about. You can do that through life insurance proceeds and trust accounts.

Hassle-Free Life Insurance

Let's start with life insurance, which can cover up a lot of financial sins and make things for your heirs super easy. Let's say you have five people in the family. A big, fat-free, lump-sum life insurance check that you can cut up like a pizza pie allows everyone to do whatever the heck they want. They want to spend it on a condo in Florida? Great. They want to join a sailing club or pay off their mortgage? Sure. They want to throw the whole lot into your grandkids' college fund? Excellent.

Let's face it. If you leave behind property, some people will have the funds to handle the upkeep and pay the taxes. Others won't. Some people are going to rake leaves. Some people aren't. Those just aren't considerations with a life insurance policy. While I'm not an estate attorney nor a tax advisor, I want to offer you a couple more basics to consider when you go talk to one.

- **Minimize Potential State or Federal Estate Tax**
  Since every state has a different set of tax laws, you may want to look into re-registering assets and titling them differently. Let's say that Linda has two million dollars of assets in her name, and Linda's husband has two million dollars in his name. In Massachusetts, each of their heirs wouldn't have to pay Massachusetts state estate tax following their deaths because each has two million dollars or less in their name titled correctly. Whereas, if that money was all under a single name, their heirs would have to pay anywhere from 0–16 percent tax on that second $2 million. That's a big deal—a significant hit to your assets and a windfall to the state. As you can see, planning ahead can save your heirs tens to hundreds of thousands in taxes.

- **A Place for All Your Stuff**
  A trust is kind of like the hold in the fishing boat that stores the harvested treasure. When you have a trust, your estate doesn't go through the probate process, which can be time-consuming, costly, and very public after you die. When setting up a trust, which can remain active for an extended period post-mortality or can be dissolved shortly after death, you transfer ownership of assets such as real estate, brokerage accounts, bank accounts, vehicles, and art collections, etc. to the trust.

While you're alive, your trust can be revocable, meaning you can change it at any time. Upon your death, it becomes an irrevocable trust, which means that your trust can't be changed by anyone for any reason. So, a trust can help ensure that your wishes, along with any promises you make, are honored.

A trust can also provide creditor protection. Since the trust is no longer legally owned by you but rather by the trustee, a creditor cannot satisfy a judgment against the assets held in that trust. And since any assets placed in a trust are not counted as part of your taxable estate, that becomes an advantage tax-wise for heirs if your state levies an estate tax and/or if your estate is valued at more than the federal exclusion amount which is currently at over $13 million individually.

A trust also allows an element of control from the grave should you want to make special allowances or impose any conditions. Since thoughts and wishes, along with designated trustees and beneficiaries, are noted ahead of death, a trust can assure that the assets you treasure and the values you deem important (education, housing, charity, etc.) are perpetuated once you're gone.

You can solve the problem of a young or irresponsible heir getting too much too fast and blowing the money. For example, you can state that Ashley receives money to pay for college, but only gets the remainder of her inheritance upon graduation, or that at a certain age, she gets a certain amount to purchase a home.

Again, you'll want to consult a legal expert when it comes to your estate planning in general and establishing trusts in specific. The fact to keep in mind, however, is that a trust can align one's values with the assets that are left behind in the trust since the terms of the trust can clearly define how the assets inherited by the beneficiaries should be managed and used. The trustee is responsible for handling that piece, and so in a sense, they then become the captain of the ship left behind by the deceased grantor who established the trust.

What Do You Want to Leave Behind?

Some folks leave a legacy of high-purposed assets like a family home, business and life insurance, or retirement accounts and trusts, to be expressly utilized and stretched for generations. Others leave a chaotic wake with no game plan, high administrative and probate costs, and an emotional struggle for their heirs. Where do you fall on that scale? What's your vision, and what's your goal? If leaving two rental homes for the kids to split or manage does little but cause strife and financially strap your heirs, your intention is ruined. Would you be better off selling both properties and, instead, arranging for your heirs to receive an income stream or asset distribution through a trust?

If you don't want to bequeath your heirs with a complicated mess, you need to figure out what you and your estate will be leaving behind if you haven't already, and then express those wishes orally and in writing. Think about how you want to ensure your legacy. Hopefully, there are some great life experiences, lessons, memories, and experiences to be shared and relished for generations because it's not *just* about the money.

Of course, assets afford us the opportunity to think a bit bigger, experience a bit more of life, and give a little more while we're alive and then after we're gone. That's why your financial habits and how you utilize the resources have always mattered more than the finances themselves. Sure, saving, earning, and investing are all critical. So is ascertaining—

and hitting—your number. That tells part of the story. But it doesn't tell the whole story. Ultimately, the number represents the life you can and do lead, what you stand for, what the assets allow you to do, and the legacy you can leave behind. But, as we've discussed, your legacy extends far beyond that.

That's why I've written a Love Letter to my family, which I shared with Joe and Chuck, my two closest childhood friends. I want those sentiments conveyed to Karen and the kids, in addition to any financial assets. At my suggestion, my friends have written their own Love Letters, which I hold in confidence, sealed in my nightstand. We all realize that leaving our family members with a final message of love is one of the most important things we can do to cement our legacies. I learned that firsthand.

The Real Legacy

My grandmother died almost penniless in subsidized, public elder housing in Florida. While she left behind little more than an old, used car, she provided a legacy of family traditions and memories that no tangible inheritance could ever replace.

Nana, who had seven children and a whole host of grandkids, was a motivating force in my life right to the end. She always had a sparkle in her eye, a smile, and an embrace, along with time for conversation and a meal together. She made me, and everyone else, feel special—that was her gift. And she shared what mattered most to her with her loved ones—time and praise.

Functioning essentially as a single mom of seven children whom she raised in the housing projects, she relied on an abundance of patience and faith to help her through. Years later, the routine of going to church every Sunday morning still meant a lot to her. So, Nana, who was also a teacher at our Sunday School, made going to church a priority for her grandkids. Every Sunday morning, she would pick up a handful of her grandchildren in her peach Ford Fairmont station wagon. And every week, she would hand each of us a quarter or two from her change purse to put into the church collection, a quiet reminder that we could always do something for others in need. Nana didn't ever have her own home after my grandfather left one afternoon never to return, nor fancy clothes, nor a vacation planned, and here she was putting the little she had in the collection basket and ensuring we did the same. I can't help but think of that every time I see or touch a quarter. I treasure that life lesson, along with all the others she shared.

Me on Nana's lap during a summer cookout.

Nana taught us to believe that we all would have a bigger, better future and that we needed to save up for that future. She's the one who took me to the local bank on my birthday while I was still in grade school to open my first passbook savings account with a $10 bill. The message was simple—you will want things in life, and you will have a job and work for them, but you need to be disciplined about taking a piece of what you have now and save it for something later. How profound.

When Nana died, she left me a bible, a handmade blanket, and a dried rose petal rosary I had brought her from Spain. She also gifted me with the promise she had made to herself not to allow a family secret to pass with her. At the time, I was 34 and a father of two with a third on the way when I received a letter saying that Charles Reed was not my father and that I needed to ask my parents about my birthright.

I felt like I had been sucker-punched. Who would tell me something like this? I didn't recognize the handwriting. My only clue was the postmark, which showed that the letter had been mailed in Tampa.

I called my grandmother, who had moved to Florida.

"Hey Nana, when you send me my birthday card every year, does it go through Tampa?"

"Oh yes," she replied in her sweet voice. "Derek, whenever I send you anything, it goes through the Tampa post office."

"Got to go," I sputtered, struggling to control my emotions. "Talk to you later."

When I called her the next day, my uncle was at her house. My uncles and my aunts lived in the same town and the next town over, as did my cousins, so there was always someone visiting, especially since we all knew by then that she was dying of bone cancer.

That was on a Sunday. Monday went by. On Tuesday night, I went down to the basement and, for the third time, called my grandmother, who was like Mother Teresa to me.

"Hey, Nana, do you have a moment?"

"Sure."

"So, is there anyone visiting you at the house?"

"No," she assured me.

I went for it. "There are three people in my life who would never lie to me," I said. "I sleep with one of them at night. The other one is my mother, who gave birth to me. And the third person is you."

"Yes," she agreed.

"So, I've got to ask you a question and I need an honest answer. Did you send me the letter?"

"What did the letter say?"

With Nana on my wedding day, July 27, 1996.

"I think you know, Nana. Did you send me the note, and is it true?"

"I did, and it's true."

We talked for the next 35 to 40 minutes. I remember looking at the basement's drop ceiling and feeling like the tiles were clouds hanging over me.

The next day I showed up at my parents' house unannounced. They were both there. We all sat down in the living room. I got right to it.

"I got this letter in the mail concerning my birthright."

"Really?" my mother countered without wasting a moment. "What did it say?"

My father put up his hand to silence her and spoke her name. Then he looked at me deadpan.

"Derek, I'm not your biological father, but you're my son," he said. "I raised you."

"You're a bigger man than I'll ever be," I said without missing a beat. "I don't know how to repay you."

"You make me proud every day," Dad replied. "That's enough for me."

Dad's values shaped me before I knew the truth about my birth as well as after. Though his life was far from steady or ideal, his moral compass was so strong that at 17 years old, he opted to invest in me even before marrying my mother and taking responsibility for the two children they would eventually have together. That's not something I'll ever be able to repay other than paying it forward.

The man who signed my birth certificate and took me on at such a young age didn't have to lift a finger for me. Apart from making me realize that I'd won the lottery, Nana's letter didn't change anything between us. I felt even more respect for my dad, who didn't go to school past the eighth grade. And I know how proud Captain Charlie is of my siblings and me and what we represent.

I hope he also knows how much he had to do with creating us. Despite being a calm, non-confrontational guy, he made it clear from early on that he wanted and expected things to be done a certain way. For us kids that meant we were to study hard and go to college in order to achieve a better, easier lifestyle. What a legacy right there!

The love we share is as deep now as it has always been. I know that's what counts the most. You can have all the money in the world, but if you don't have a loving, caring family and people with whom to share your joys and obstacles, you've got nothing.

Ironically, Nana's decision to tell me the truth before she died led to me gaining a new family—and a new model of strength and integrity—even as I mourned her loss. My mom had asked my biological dad, Valdor Jr., not to interject himself into my life as I went through the important stages of school, college, marriage, business, and raising a family. She feared that contact might throw me off course mentally or emotionally. So, from a distance, Val watched me grow and mature in our native city of Gloucester, MA. I'm sure that attending sporting events to see me compete as the captain of both my high school football and track teams, knowing that I was his son—his creation—filled him with as much pain as it did pride. But he kept his promise to let my mom reveal the truth at her time and inclination. While that's not exactly how it all played out, I'm not sure I could have done what he did for a day, much less for 34-plus years. And that, too, has created a legacy that will forever be with me. And now, thanks to my Nana, Val is a part of my life.

Valdor (Val) Burgess, Jr. and Charlie Reed, my two dads and real-life heroes.

Dad and Val's legacies are still being built on an already rock-solid foundation of nobility, honor, and responsibility. What more could I ever ask for? I did my part by accepting as a mature adult the facts of my birth and upbringing.

All these years later, gratitude still shapes how I live my life and how I do business. As it turns out, I'm the product of three teen parents. I'm the product of Head Start. I know what government cheese tastes like. And I came out the other end, thanks in no small measure to my folks who took care of me even though the man I consider to be my father certainly didn't have to. How can I not give back and pass that on to my kids and others? How can I not encourage people and create opportunities for them to make a difference in areas that are important to them and that will cement their legacy?

As the saying goes, no one has ever gone to the cemetery with a U-Haul behind the hearse. At a certain point, when you know you have enough for you and your heirs to be comfortable, it becomes less about how much you have and more about what you're going to leave behind. In many cases, it doesn't take millions of dollars to make an impact.

That sentiment is reflected in Beauport Financial Services. We believe in giving back. As a firm, we're charitably minded and community-focused, so we contribute annual grants of up to $5,000 each to nonprofit causes that our clients care about. We do this by setting aside 10 percent of our profits every year. Since its inception in 2005, our Richard D. Wilson Community Response Gift Fund has awarded hundreds of dollars to stellar civic and nonprofit organizations. Cutting checks to charities and funding coats and mittens and hats for kids whose family can't afford those necessities inspires us and inspires our teams.

We're on a mission to create $100 million of charitable capital over the next 10 years. Even if we fall a little bit short, that's still an awesome and worthy pursuit that will benefit lots of folks. But what if every financial advisor did this, and we all were responsible for encouraging clients to think a little differently and carve out a piece for someone else? That little ripple becomes a wave of goodness that could really make an impact.

As we get along in life, we're all fishing for something that matters to us. At Beauport, we believe that we should always leave something behind, especially if we have others we love and care about, so we model that. Of course, you can't possibly feel confident and competent about giving money away while you're in your sixties unless you've done a really good job of planning and have a game plan showing you that you can safely do so. Take comfort knowing that while life will present both opportunities and challenges, you're prepared and ready for them, you've got a process and a game plan, there's a captain in your financial wheelhouse, you stand for something meaningful while you're alive, and your legacy is going to matter when you're no longer here. That's a voyage worthy of pursuit. Congratulations!

CATCH OF THE DAY:

- Invest for life (yours and any heirs), learn along the way, and share your wisdom and gratitude with others. Hopefully, your assets will endure after you're gone, so be sure to communicate your plan with your heirs.
- Even when you know the patterns, the weather, have the correct equipment, and the skill set, you still must get to work and follow the game plan. What season are you in? Are you still fishing for retirement (capital accumulation mode), have you landed and prepped the fish, and then figured out your best way home, or are you already on your way back to the dock (decumulation/distribution mode), aspiring to make the most of your resources to finish with great purpose and clarity? Identifying which stage you are in is just as important as knowing where you want to finish.
- Honor the work that has resulted in your bounty—protect it and help ensure that your wishes are respected by setting up a trust with a message to your heirs to let them know what you care about to attach meaning to the money.

CONCLUSION

OVER THE YEARS, THANKS TO DAD, I've learned that there are many ways to fish and many fish to fish for. We are all fishing for something as we search for purpose in life—better professional opportunity, financial independence or early retirement, a balanced and healthy lifestyle of work/family/play, funding our children's educations properly, starting or transitioning a business, retiring all debt, creating an enhanced income stream, living well and protecting what's taken a lifetime to accumulate for the next generation, planning for philanthropy, etc. To make that work, we need a captain and a compass to help us to follow a reliable, predictable process that spells out not only the goal but also contingencies for when something goes astray. Then we need to implement that plan, and monitor it along the way, expecting rough seas as we go.

Having people with the right values to oversee all that can make all the difference. As I've learned rather recently, two captains can guide and care for the ship as long as they're both pulling in the same direction.

The man I call my hero in life, my dad Captain Charlie, provided me with a great example of strength, optimism, preparation, and determination, all of that done without fanfare by a resilient, honorable, and quietly remarkable man. Bringing me up as his son taught me about honor, persistence, and commitment. Even before I knew I wasn't his biological child, I witnessed him willingly take the wheel and do the best he could.

Meanwhile, my mother, my rock, captained our home-front during the weeks Dad was away. Their shared goal and desire for me and my brighter future helped mold the man I have become and continues to play an important role in my family and personal life.

My biological father, Valdor, having promised my mother that he would let her tell me the details of my birth at a time and place of her choosing, may have taken a backseat, but he was always there in the background and able to step in if needed or asked. There could be no better example of patience, respect, and honor. I sensed his deep caring immediately upon meeting him for the first time in September 2006.

To think that this whole new facet of my life came to be upon the passing of Nana, my biggest cheerleader in life, who was penniless on the asset sheet but abundantly rich in what she gave me while here!

I look back on the life these four incredible family members created for me based on the values they stood for, and I know what it means to walk the walk, talk the talk, and live a life worth living. And now I get to help people live their values.

"I want to donate and make a difference," they tell me. "Can you help me do that?" Those conversations make me want to pinch myself. They're helping me live *my* why.

So, what's your why?

Determining what matters most to you—your values—will help you figure out how and why you want to invest, and then help you enjoy the journey along the way. But you can't do that if you're just looking to get to the destination and not paying attention to the beauty—or to the process—as you sail through life's stages.

Sure, the accumulation phase is essential. But greed isn't. We all fight time clocks and the calendar, but there's a time to fish and a time to ensure that there will be enough left for next time. In the meantime, you need to make sure you develop a healthy relationship with money early on or change the one you have now. Whether you're making a little or a lot, you need to live on 80 percent, save 10 percent, and invest 10 percent.

Distribution mode kicks in once you've reached the dock. By then, you've measured the bounty, so now it's all about getting the best possible return in a way that ensures you'll be able to do it all over again next time.

Knowing what season you're in as an investor will help you determine just what that process looks like. Are you still an income seeker? Or are you a retiree looking to create wealth? This is where fishing becomes an art form, and I get to take poetic license when it comes to filling the boat. Creative, strategic planning for retirement income, asset preservation, and legacy concerns all help define the process to follow, always keeping the end game in mind.

Still, certain basics remain constant. The boat is safe and tidy, well equipped, it has left the dock, you've inspected the fishing spot with your crew, you're on the fish (not just any species of fish by the way—the exact fish you have set out to catch), and you've landed the fish. Now what do you do with all this fish? Get it on board, get it dressed and stored in the hold properly so that you get the best price for it when it hits the dock. No matter what, the goal *always* is to get home safe and sound, and if the catch is plentiful, even better—a great addition to the fish stories, the experience, and the memories.

Is there risk involved? Sure. It's called fishing—not catching—for a reason. Sometimes you do come up empty, but you continue to cast a line, set a net, and move around the vast ocean of financial opportunity. Without hooks or that net in the water, there is no bounty.

So why venture out and take the risk of putting your hard-earned assets into something that may not work out? Leave your savings in the bank or under your proverbial pillow for safekeeping, and it will always be there, right? Not really. As we've discussed, you also have to factor in the huge risks of inflation, which keeps increasing day-to-day costs, putting you in danger of outliving your assets. And don't forget about the taxman, your silent business partner in all things fruitful and profitable. Only by taking calculated risks can you outpace those risks.

Besides, a little stress and risk promote growth. Consider the grapevine. With less water, the root system grows deeper and more extensive as the plant searches for water and nourishment, and the vines produce richer, more concentrated fruit, which will turn into a great wine provided the winemaker knows what to do with the grapes. Similarly, a talented financial advocate who knows what to do with the ship and crew can steer you clear of—or through—trouble and look for sound opportunities with your assets along the way.

It's not always perfect or pretty during the voyage, but a calm inevitably follows life's obstacles and financial storms. Your goal is to endure, to see the next sunny day and, if you cannot, to ensure that your loved ones and heirs fully enjoy it in your stead.

In the end, two questions rise above all the rest.

1. What do you stand for?
2. How did you define success?

If you did your fishing and did it wisely, you'll enjoy the harvest during the final stage of your life, leave something behind that reflects what you stood for, and make sure that the lessons, as well as the assets, get passed along to the people and causes you care about.

Here's to your kind of success. Fish on!

ABOUT THE AUTHOR

Karen and me, and from left to right, Jeremy, Nathan, and Katherine, with our 10-year-old Golden Retriever, Lincoln.

Every Ship Requires a Captain
About Your Financial Captain, Derek Reed

I'm a wealth planner with specialty designations in the investment and insurance planning fields, vigorously earned to best serve our aspiring and currently successful retirees as a managing partner at Beauport Financial Services.

About the Author

I am one incredibly blessed man that's for sure—a proud native son of a Gloucester commercial fishing family and a product of steadfast teenaged parents who are still committed to one another and their family 52 years later. Raised in a gritty, loving, and supportive community with amazing friends, extended family, and many wise mentors, I am as committed to my family as my parents are to theirs. Just like the ocean beyond Gloucester Harbor provided opportunity to my dad, the sword captain, I was always encouraged to dream, to travel, and to seek meaningful experiences over the A. Piatt Andrew Bridge leading out of town. But my roots, a growing business, and my family ground me to this special place on the North Shore of Boston.

Captaining the financial ships of big-hearted, caring clients is the biggest responsibility and honor. At Beauport, we care about you and we believe deeply in the Golden Rule, which leads us to support the local communities of Cape Ann and beyond with our company Donor Advised Fund.

Discover more about how we help you retire with confidence and how we serve our community at beauportfinancial.com.